The Role of Norms in U.S. State-building Following the End of the Cold War

Ryan Sonneville

Table of Contents

Chapter 1:
Introduction

On September 11th, 1990, George H.W. Bush addressed

Congress as the United States entered the Gulf War. He

contended that the world was experiencing a change in norms and

practices that would have long term effects on how the

international community governed itself. The President stated that

"out of these troubled times…a new world order – can emerge: a

new era – freer from the threat of terror, stronger in the pursuit of

justice, and more secure in the quest for peace" (Hass, 2005). As

the Cold War came to an end, there appeared to be justifiable

reason to believe that the world order articulated by the President

would come to be. Yet, the subsequent decade demonstrated the

limitations of this celebratory rhetoric, as the 1990s saw a

significant increase in the number of states experiencing civil war

(Fearon and Laitin, 2004, p.10). The United Nations saw a dramatic increase in the number of peace keeping operations (PKO) it spearheaded in the 1990s as well. Between 1948 and 1987, the UN Security Council authorized just thirteen peacekeeping missions; between 1988 and 2004, they have authorized over forty-five (Fearon and Laitin, 2004, p.10), including nineteen "complex peace operations" intended to create self-sustaining state institutions (Englebert and Tull, 2008, p.106).

Since the end of the Cold War, state-building has become more common. Allowing predominantly Western nations the right to administer over other states was a common practice in the colonial era, but had fallen out of favour after the end of the Second World War (Oisin, 2009, p.15). Most of the pre-1988 interventions were classic peacekeeping operations, in which international forces monitored a border or cease-fire line following an interstate war (Fearon and Laitin, 2004, p.11). Many of the peace-building operations post-1988 can be described as state-building exercises[1], whereas an international authority

---

[1] State-building and nation-building are often used interchangeably in literature on this subject, although there are differences between them. For the purpose of this paper, Simon Chesterman's definitions of state-building (building the "highest institutions of governance in a territory") and nation-building (the creation of

(principally, through the UN) constructs or reconstructs "institutions of governance capable of providing citizens with physical and economic security" (Chesterman, 2004, p.5). This often requires that the foreign power takes on roles traditionally allocated to domestic authorities, such as building social and governmental institutions, training police forces, and constructing functioning justice systems (Chesterman, 2004, p.5). Many of the recent state-building operations can be considered transitional administrations, insofar as the mandate given to the foreign authority is temporary, with the intention that the "powers of the state" be returned to domestic leaders in the future (Chesterman, 2004, p.5).

With the sheer number of state-building operations carried out since the end of the Cold War, and with a recent shift in the international discourse towards interventionism (Wheeler, 2000, p.286; Olesen, 2005, p.109), examining modern state-building operations is an important endeavour. What is striking concerning many state-building missions carried out by the UN and the U.S. is how these projects change and adapt over time. In Kosovo,

---

"a people who share common customs, origins, history") will be employed (Chesterman, 2004, p.4).

Iraq, and Afghanistan, the foreign-run transitional authority's degree of intervention and interference into the domestic workings of the host state fluctuated. In these three cases, the mandate, aims, and resources allocated did not remain static throughout the operation's duration. This presents an important question that has implications for the study of policy evolution: when do transitional administrations led by the United States become more committed, both militarily and politically, in a state-building project in the post-Cold War, and when do these administrations adopt a more limited approach allocating more authority to domestic actors with a lighter foreign footprint?

To tackle these questions, the United States' two most recent state-building endeavours, Afghanistan and Iraq, will be examined. As noted previously, state-building operations often change throughout the duration of the project, therefore these operations will be divided into separate case studies to examine how the level of intervention changed from one stage to another. The separate stages of the state-building process are not chosen arbitrarily, but reflect a specific and notable policy change reflecting a transformation from a previous phase. How U.S.

policymakers view the norms and rules that govern their actions considerably affects their state-building policies in Iraq and Afghanistan. Policymakers responsible for the early stages of the state-building process in both countries conceived of these operations through an overly-materialist lens. As these policies failed to bring about an acceptable result to the U.S. government, a new theoretical framework was employed that carried with it its own set of norms and policy options. Additionally, the UN state-building missions in Kosovo will be examined. This UN-led operation was extensive in its aims, and this operation demonstrates how a separate set of norms within a transitional institution can produce alternative policy options and objectives.

Methodology

This paper will use a few methodologies concurrently. Mainly, it will adopt a comparative case study approach, focusing on positive cases that demonstrate how a change in norms begets changes in policy (Ragin, 2004, p.125). All three cases represent an attempt by a foreign authority to rebuild and reorganize a state's institutional structures following a major combat operation in the post-Cold War world, providing ample parallels and discrepancies between these undertaking. The Afghan and Iraqi cases are the two most recent U.S. state-building projects and the most extensive missions undertaken by the U.S. since the end of the Cold War. While both the Iraqi and Afghan state-building projects were justified and executed with different rationales, both share an analogous policy trend and are thus discussed concurrently. Comparing the two U.S. cases to a recent UN state-building operation also reveals how policymakers socially construct the norms with which they conceptualize these operations, resulting in different policy prescriptions. Each state-building case will be broken down into two or three stages, allowing changes in the foreign transitional authority's policy to be observed within the cases.

This dissertation builds upon two theoretical models: the "soft" constructivism pioneered by Alexander Wendt and the discursive institutionalism (DI) of Vivien Schmidt (Kratochwil, 2003, p.24). While Wendt's work is generally concerned with the relations between states and international society, its theoretical foundation can be applied to all social interactions that produce norms and rules (Wendt, 1999, p.5). Studies that examine state-building projects often focus on specific "design questions" such as the raw materials, resources, and blueprints used to advance each project (Etzioni, 2009-2010). While conceding that materialist variables do contribute to specific norms and policy perspectives, I affirm that "the role of ideas" in shaping structures and policy is an equally important factor that affects the way actors behave (Wendt, 1999, p.5). Habitually absent from the study of state-building operations are the norms and perceived rules guiding policymakers when they advance a specific plan of action. How policymakers conceive international society, view its structure and limits, and the foreign authority's responsibility in a state-building exercise result from a shared framework "constraining and shaping behaviour" (Copeland, 2006, p.3). In this sense, I adopt Wendt's casual epistemological position as well as his constitutive ontology, focusing on empirically verifiable actions while maintaining the ontological foundation that "structures constitute agents and rules" (Wendt, 1999, p.90).

Explicit in Wendt's assertion that "anarchy is what states make of it" and Schmidt's declaration that "ideas and discourse matter," is a shared contention that norms and outlooks influence how states and institutions operate (Wendt, 1992, pg.395; Copeland, 2006, p.3). Based on different perspectives and separate ontological "starting points," states produce different decisions based on the rules and norms that they perceive to govern action (Wendt, 1999, p.6). Norms, in this sense, are contested: they struggle with competing norms for dominance (Florini, 1996, p.364). Discursive institutionalism builds on constructivist precepts, and it applies these norms based on an understanding of action to institutions and organizations. By examining the "construction and reconstruction of political interests and values" within an organization responsible for a state-building operation, one observes how normative rules built into institutions explain that institution's actions (Schmidt, 2008, p.305). Additionally, DI recognizes that agents and structures are "mutually constitutive"; that is, individual agents are both constrained by the norms and logic of the institution they work within, and they also contribute to an institution's evolution as the actor works within them (Schmidt, 2008, p.315) (see Figure 1). The ideas and perspectives individuals bring to an institution matter, and normative guidelines are debated within policymaking organizations, just as these ideas are at the state and international levels. This means that action cannot be examined on one systemic level alone, and that a holistic methodological approach must be used to comprehend changes in a state-building operation.

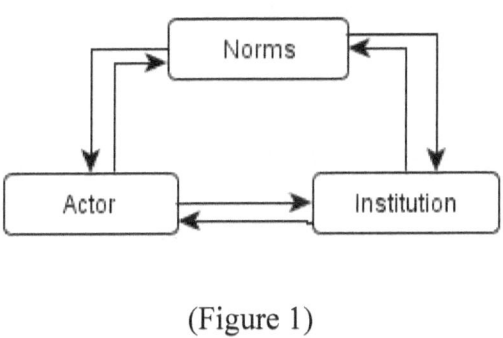

(Figure 1)

When discussing each stage of the state-building process, the following model will be used (see Figure 2). The independent variables measured in this paper are the norms imbedded in the foreign institution responsible for a state-building exercise. The intervening variables are the institutions created by the transitional authority, such as justice systems and security apparatuses. The dependent variable is the perceived result of these institutions and policies on the host state. The norms

13

imbedded in each stage of the state-building project (the independent variable) will produce a set of institutions (the independent variable), that generates an observable and measurable effect (the dependent variable). If the foreign authority believes the institutional models and approach to state-building have failed, it may produce a change in norms that then results in a separate institutional approach. The change in the transitional administration's policy between each stage of the process is where the theory takes precedent; this change helps explain those undertaken in each overarching case.

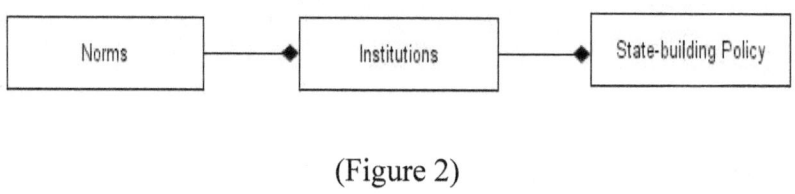

(Figure 2)

Chapter 2:
The Theoretical Foundation of
International Society and State-building

Before these state-building cases can be examined, a brief history of the normative changes surrounding international society, sovereignty, and state-building is essential in comprehending the normative dimension of these projects. An international society exists "when a group of states, conscious of certain common interests and common values, form a society in the sense that they conceive themselves to be bound by a common set of rules in their relations with one another" (Bull, 1977, p.13). Within this conception of international society, there are two divergent standards. Firstly, the Pluralist tradition allows for various classifications of "good" governance and modes of social operation (Wheeler, 2000, p.27). In principle, the international society should be governed by a respect for state sovereignty

(Clark, p.153). Secondly, Solidarists argue that individuals are the beneficiaries of rights, not states (Wheeler, 2000, p.11). States in this international society have a "moral responsibility to protect their citizens," and a state may lose the right to govern in this society if it infringes on the rights of its citizens, resulting in the "use of force to stop the oppression" (Wheeler, 2000, p.12-13). Intervention on behalf of an endangered people is thus a "moral duty" of members of the international society (Wheeler, 2000, p.13). These competing conceptions of society are at the heart of the debate surrounding international society and state-building.

Following the Rwandan genocide and the war in Bosnia, then UN Secretary-General Boutros Boutros-Ghali released a supplement to his paper titled "Agenda for Peace." The supplement recognized that a new breed of interstate conflicts had arisen, as these conflicts were "accompanied by the collapse of state institutions, especially the police and judiciary," requiring international intervention to expand beyond traditional military and humanitarian tasks to include the "promotion of national reconciliation and the re-establishment of effective government" (Chesterman, 2007, p.5; UN, 1995, p.5). In light of this, the

Secretary-General continued to maintain that the UN should approach nation building projects that impose state institutions on foreign peoples with caution (UN, 1995, p.13-14). Despite Boutros-Ghali's warning, the UN engaged in a slew of state-building exercises in subsequent years, taking significant control over the construction of institutions in the host state, culminating in the UN missions in Kosovo and East Timor, where the transitional administrations where given effective sovereignty (Chesterman, 2007, p.5).

The prevailing thoughts on sovereignty following the end of European colonialism were that equality between states and people in the international system was necessary in order to bring about a more just international system than preceding one. The equality established in this new system demanded, "that persons be treated equally insofar as they [were] regarded as equals" (Bain, 2003, p.61), and this understanding of impartiality provided the norms and general framework for the relations between states in the post-colonial era. This conception of liberty entails the right of an entity to be treated as an equal by others, regardless of their capacity. Stuart Mill's position that an individual "cannot rightfully be compelled" to act in a certain manner, even if it is supposed to make them happier and more secure, was the outlook employed on the international level, granting all states the right to govern their societies as they saw fit (Mill, 1859, p.13).

This was a major shift in norms away from the previous colonial era. Colonialism was not simply a push for resources; it was conceived as "a divine plan for the salvation of the pagans, as a secular mandate to 'civilize' the 'barbarians' or 'savages,' as a 'white man's burden' that he is privileged to carry" (Osterhammel, 1995, p.16). These influential states believed that they were responsible for civilizing "less advanced" people and were moreover "convinced of their own superiority and their ordained mandate to rule" (Osterhammel, 1995, p.17). This perceived superiority of advanced Western states was not regulated to proponents of overt colonial endeavours. Karl Marx argued that Great Britain had a responsibility to its Indian subjects to bestow upon them the foundations of Western society while annihilating "old Asiatic society" (Marx, 1853, p.132). P.H. Kerr held that superior civilizations had a duty to administer those who did not posses the personal ability to govern themselves effectively "until they are able to take their place alongside more advanced peoples" (Kerr, 1916, p.149; Bain, 2003, p.61). While Marx, Kerr, and the colonizers before them were informed by separate ideologies and political objectives, they shared a common conception of an international society: advanced nations had a duty to civilize and modernize less advanced civilizations.

It was not until the post-colonial era that the principles of unconditional equality extended to all people and states. The era was articulated in the United Nations Assembly Resolutions 421 (V) and 545 (VI), affirming the importance of self-determination for all people and nations, bestowing upon them the right to "freely determine their political status and freely pursue their economic, social, and cultural development" (UN General Assembly, 1950). Declaration on the Granting of Independence to Colonial Countries and Peoples (Resolution 1514 (XV) further illustrates the governing principles that would direct international society through the pos-colonial years. This declaration stated that the "denial of independence precluded the full enjoyment of fundamental human rights and that colonialism itself, no matter how Enlightened" (Bain, 2003, p.66). An international hierarchy based on a state's level of development was no longer applicable to the relations between states, and thus trusteeship was no longer considered a viable policy alternative. As Kwame Nkrumah argued, trusteeship was nothing more than a policy of "deception, hypocrisy, oppression, and exploitation" with a more acceptable moniker (Nkrumah, 1962, p.35). Since this society stressed coexistence as its governing principle, this period can accurately be described as Pluralist (Buzan, 2004, p.142).

With the end of the Cold War, rhetoric and norms concerning governance began to visibly change. At the Conference on Security and Cooperation in Europe (CSCE) in 1990, a host of states passed the 'Charter of Paris on Europe,' which unequivocally affirmed that democracy was the only form of acceptable government in modern society (CSCE, 1990, p.3). State failure in Somalia and genocide in Rwanda demonstrated a significant quandary with an international system that bestowed the same rights on all states, and an "alternative ethics to independence" began to develop (Bain, 2003, p.68). Kofi Annan, then Secretary-General of the UN, attempted to reinterpret and challenge non-interference in a sovereign state's affairs as a guiding principle of the UN. He wrote, "The Charter protects the sovereignty of peoples. It was never meant as a licence for governments to trample on human rights and human dignity. Sovereignty implies responsibility, not just power" (Annan, 1998a, p.3). While the UN Charter defended the right of states to govern without fear of foreign intervention into their domestic politics, the Universal Declaration of Human Rights bestowed upon each individual the right to liberty and freedom, and the freedom from slavery and the right to "an effective remedy" to a violation of said individual's fundamental rights (UN UDHR, 1948, Art.3,8). Even though the UN was not given explicit provisions to enforce these rights (Bull, 1977, p.83-84), scholars like Hersch Lauterpacht alleged that the inclusion of individual rights into an international governing body was a major step in the solidarist's direction, with the potential for the enforcement of these norms possible through extended interpretation (Lauterpacht, 1975, p.166-167). Martin Wright would later argue that it was individual men, not states, that were members of the international society, justifying intervention into the affairs of others as a "duty of fellow-feeling and cooperation" (Wright, 1991, p.215,116). While many scholars and statesmen continued to adhere to the pluralist conception of international society, there was a significant shift towards Solidarist norms. Morton Halperin stated that constitutional, democratic government upholding the basic standards of human rights had become the norm that now governed the society of states (Halperin, 1993, p.105). As these new norms took root, they established new ways in which states could intervene into foreign state affairs "to modify the content of other norms" (Flynn and Farrell, 1999, p.523).

In President George W. Bush's 2002 National Security Strategy, it unequivocally asserted that "freedom is the non-negotiable demand of human dignity" (NSS, 2002, p.vi) and that the United States must use its power to advance a global policy that "favours freedom" (NSS, 2002, p.25). The document exemplified a move in American foreign policy towards conditional relations between states, arguing, "accountability must be expected and required" (NSS, 2002, p.vi). These arguments, coming both from academics, theorists, and policymakers, reflect a change in U.S. perceptions towards an outlook closer to Solidarism than Pluralism (Press-Barnathan, 2004, p.208). By placing an emphasis on the rights of individuals over states, it allows the U.S. to "exercise power in such a way that it remedies the imperfect moral and material state in which a portion of the human family subsists" (Bain, 2003, p.65). Interference with a state's domestic affairs was thus justified on the grounds that it will improve the lives of citizens in the troubled state while furthering U.S. interests in maintaining international stability (Dworkin, 1971, p.108; Krauthammer, 2004, p.15).

The UN carried out two of the most ambitious state-building projects in 1999, first in Kosovo (UNMIK) and then in East Timor (UNTAET), with both projects appearing to signal the "demise of the ethics of post-colonial international society and along with it the principle of universal equality" (Bain, 2003, p.69) These nation-building projects, often described as neo-trusteeships, placed a large degree of authority in the hands of UN officials, providing them with a mandate to implement the mission's agenda that far exceeded previous UN state-building missions after the Cold War (Caplan, 2005, p.19). In both cases, the UN created transitional authorities that were autonomous from local control, granting itself the "powers of the state on a temporary basis" (Chesterman, 2004, pg. 5). Conditional support and recognition made their way into formal policies on aid and reconstruction efforts as well. In recent years, the international development community began to see aid as a tool to transforming conflict dynamics by withholding support and resources until improved governance was demonstrated by the recipient (UNDG, 2004, p.16). The establishment of "good government" in the state-building process became the norm (Grindle, 2002, p.28).

Chapter 3:
Case Study - UN State-building: Kosovo (UNMIK 1999-2008)

Stage 1: UNMIK 1999-2000

Following the end of the NATO-led conflict between the Federal Republic of Yugoslavia and Kosovo separatists, the UN Security Council established the most extensive and comprehensive foreign transitional authority seen in the last thirty years. Unlike in Bosnia, the UN established a peace deal and mandate not through mutual acceptance by indigenous parties, but by imposing the UN's will on the warring parties (Mertus, 2001). UNMIK's mandate would make significant reforms to Kosovo's legal and justice systems, allowing UN administrators the ability to implement policies without the support of domestic actors (something unthinkable in the previous decades). In its first regulation, the UNMIK unequivocally stated that "all legislative and executive authority with respect to Kosovo, including the administration of the judiciary, is vested in UNMIK and is

exercised by the Special Representative of the Secretary-General"
(Chesterman, 2004, p.126). The UNMIK mission was separated
into four distinct pillars, each led by an international agency
specializing in one area of the state-building process, and with a
unified chain of command headed by a Special Representative of
the UN Secretary General (SRSG) (Oisin, 2009, p.113). While the
UNMIK's mandate was extensive, it also created a dilemma: the
transitional authority exercised a high level of control over the
creation of domestic institutions, yet promoted local ownership of
these institutions in preparation for self-rule (Narten, 2009,
p.264). UNMIK oversaw the creation of local institutions such as
fiscal, taxation, and housing authorities, with the Kosovan
controlled Joint Interim Administrative Structure (JIAS), but
domestic authorities had little real power over the institution's
character (Ibid, p.265).

While international police were brought in to provide
security, Kosovan judges and prosecutors retained exclusive
authority over the administration of justice (Hartmann, 2003, p.1).
A fifty-thousand-strong NATO-led military force was created
(KFOR), pulling troops from thirty countries (Wilson, 2006,

p.153). The UN mission took a radical turn and broke with previous precedents by appointing international judges and prosecutors (IJP) to Kosovo's district courts; eventually the courts were granted the ability to take on any case, even after the case had been assigned to a Kosovan jurist (Hartmann, 2003, p. 2). In previous "heavy footprint" nation building projects like the United Nations Mission in Bosnia Herzegovina (UNMIBH), international judges and prosecutors were "limited to assistance, monitoring, or oversight," and they did not act within the domestic judicial system (Ibid, p. 2).

Initially, indigenous Kosovan prosecutors and judges administrated over the legal system (Ibid, p.4). The UN quickly found that the jurists appointed to work in the country's legal system were deficient for a number of reasons. Most of the jurists working in judiciary throughout the 1990s were seen as collaborators with an oppressive regime. Many Kosovan jurists were removed from the judiciary with the 1989 elimination of Kosovo's autonomy by Milosevic's government, which disbanded the country's independent Supreme Court, Provincial Prosecutors Office, and legislature (Perriello, 2006, p.9). Those jurists who were untainted from collaboration had no experience in the judiciary or Prosecutor's Office (Hartmann, 2003, p.5).

Following hundreds of inter-ethnic attacks in 1999 against minority groups in Kosovo, the UNMIK found that there was a noteworthy inconsistency in how the law was being applied by the predominantly Albanian Kosovan judiciary. When KLA members were apprehended for attacks on Serbs, prosecutors would propose their release, which would then be carried out by the investigative judge (Hartmann, 2003, p.5). Additionally, SRSG had issued regulations in September 1999, which gave the transitional regime the ability to discipline judges and prosecutors for misconduct, but failed to do so (Ibid, p. 6). By the start of 2000 the UN recognized that the Kosovo justice system had considerable problems, and that the mono-ethnic Albanian Kosovan makeup of the judiciary appeared to discriminate against Serbs, giving the local Serb population less incentive to work with both local and foreign authorities (Ibid). Ethnic bias was not the only problem facing the predominately Albanian Kosovan judiciary: community pressure and threats of violence against the indigenous authorities played a significant role in the judiciary's corruptive practices (Hartmann, p.7). Coercion of Kosovan judges and prosecutors "spanned the spectrum from gentle phone hints by those in power, to threats of bodily harm against the judge or his or her family" (Ibid, p.7). Major changes to the country's legal system had to be made if the UN's goals were going to be achieved.

The norms inherent in UNMIK's mandate and authority are represented by numerous statements and articles made by UN leaders and policymakers. In 1999, Kofi Annan argued that individuals needed more than words, "they [needed] a real and sustained commitment to help end their cycles of violence, and give them a new chance to achieve peace and prosperity" (Annan, 1999a). He added that the UN was more willing to intervene in the affairs of sovereign states then they had in the past (Annan, 1999a). Implicit in UNMIK's mandate is the concept of human security developed by the UN in 1994. In 1994, the UNDP stated that human security sees "democracy, human rights, and good governance [as] indivisible," and the UN began pursuing these objectives in its state-building projects (Paris, 2004, p.24). To achieve human security goals, a more robust form of state-building had to be carried out. Simply maintaining physical security in the state would not necessarily produce democratic and liberal institutions in Kosovo. The UNDP asserted that future state-building projects needed to involve themselves with security concerns not directly connected to military matters and that forceful intervention in the early stages was desirable to more costly intervention later (UNDP, 2004, p.22). These normative precepts visibly shaped the UN's approach in Kosovo, as demonstrated by later stages.

Stage 2: UNMIK 2000-2002

There was not a momentous change in norms between the first and second stages, but political and security concerns in Kosovo during this period did reaffirm the UN's willingness to progressively intervene in the state's indigenous institutions. The first municipal elections held in October of 2000, and the Kosovo Assembly elections in November of 2001, demonstrated the highly interventionist role the UN played in the state-building process during the second stage. This process culminated in

Kosovo's preliminary constitution issued by the SRSG's office without a domestic authority to authorize it (Narten, 2009, p.265).

Recognizing the need to make adjustments to its judicial system, the transitional authority in Kosovo during its second stage saw preliminary integration of IJP into the country's legal system with the appointment of two IJP in February of 2000. By December of that year, the number of IJP increased from two to thirteen. This was an unparalleled move by the UN. Previously, international judges and prosecutors operated in a separate court system than local officials (the International Criminal Tribunal for Rwanda and the International Criminal Tribunal of Yugoslavia being prime examples). ICPs were traditionally used to prosecute individuals from the countries of the accused and were regulated to legal proceedings regarding crimes against humanity (Hartmann, 2003, p.8). The ICPs in Kosovo, however, "had the same criminal jurisdiction as any other Kosovan district judge or prosecutor" (Ibid, p.8); this jurisdiction allowed them to take on criminal cases in Kosovo. Additionally, the ICP could take a pending investigation or case away from a Kosovan judge or prosecutor if they believed local officials were unable to carry out the law adequately and justly. Initially, the ICP were only appointed in the District of Mitrovica, but following a prison strike by Serbs who alleged the law was being applied unfairly to the Serbian population, the UNMIK enacted Regulation 2000/34, which expanded the scope of the ICP to all five districts in Kosovo (Ibid, p.9).

The UN found this intrusion to be well founded following a terrorist attack on Serbian civilians outside a grocery store in Cernica, an attack resulting in the murder of three Serbs. Eyewitnesses implicated an ex-KLA member in the attack, but the Kosovan prosecutor failed to "submit questions to the alibi witness proposed by the defense," and then abandoned the case completely, arguing that it was not grounded on fact (Hartmann, 2003, p.9). Intervention by the UNMIK overturned the domestic Kosovan legal authorities.

Additionally, past failures by the UN to accept concrete authority in the early stages of a state-building or peace-keeping operation weighed heavily over the Kosovan process. The inability of the 1994 UN mission in Rwanda (UNAMIR) to stop the country's genocide was seen as a horror the UN could not repeat (Wheeler, 2000, p.214). In Rwanda, UN peacekeepers did not have the right to impose any agreement on warring groups in the state, and as soon as there was a violation of the ceasefire by either side, the UN's mandate to intervene in hostilities evaporated (Ibid, p.214). Kofi Annan later argued that "Rwanda showed us how terrible the consequences of inaction can be in the face of mass murder," and that the obstacle to necessary intervention was reluctance by Members States "to pay the human and other costs of intervention" (Annan, 1999a; Annan, 1999b, p.21). The UN appeared to take this lesson seriously, as the level of international soldiers and police officers present in the country during the first two years of the state-building operation were high (Jones et al, 2005, p.33).

The UN had learned from its failures in the 1990s, and these failures provided commitment to the Kosovo state-building operation unseen in the preceding decades. The first two years of reconstruction in Kosovo dwarfed the U.S. missions in Iraq and Afghanistan in the per capita aid provided to those countries (see Figure 3). Far more troops and international police officers were deployed to Kosovo than were to Iraq and Afghanistan, based on the size of the state and its population (Jones et al, 2005, p.183). The UN appeared to have adopted the Solidarist, conditional framework to its state-building operations, asserting that inadequate commitment to a reconstruction effort was unacceptable following a failure to adequately deal with troubles in Rwanda, Somalia, and Bosnia. However, subsequent stages of the process demonstrated rifts within the UN and its transitional authority in Kosovo.

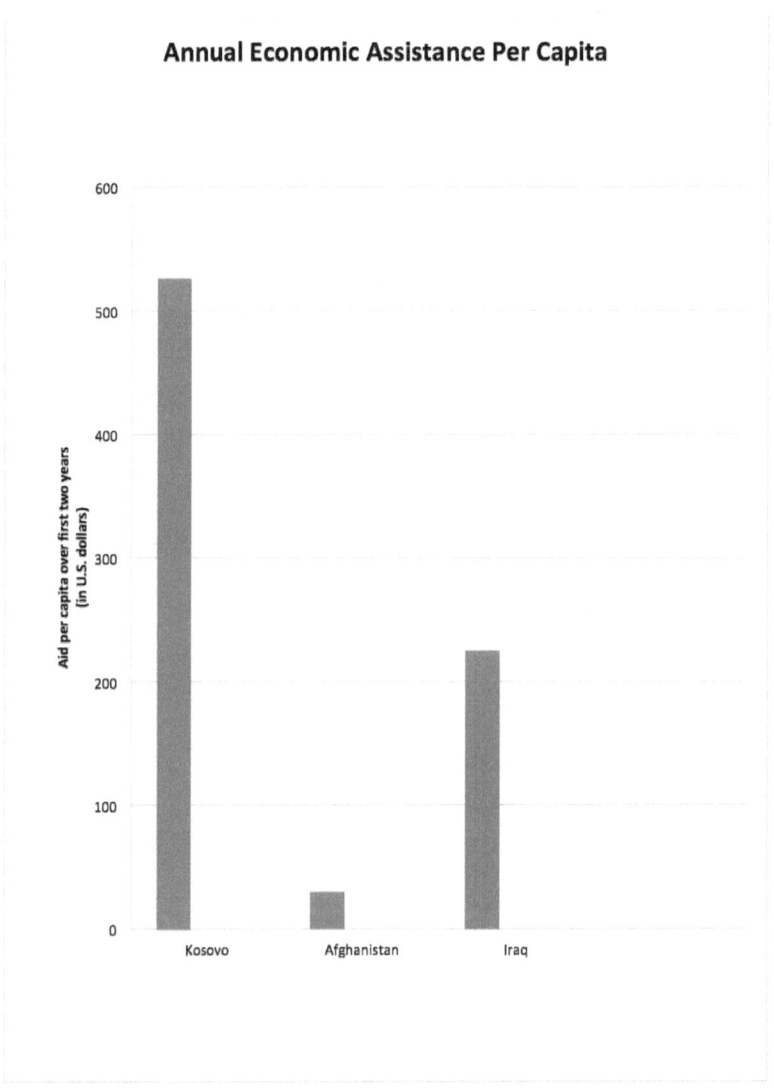

(Figure 3) (Source: Jones et al, 2005, p.182, Dobbins et al, 2005, p.xxviii)

Stage 3: UNMIK 2003-2008

In December of 2003, Harri Holkeri took command of the UNMIK. He argued that the mission's policy was inconsistent with its aims of building self-sustaining institutions (Narten, 2009, p.265). He altered the UNMIK's strategy, adopting a cooperative approach that worked with indigenous authorities to develop and implement the UN mandate's framework (Narten, 2009, p.265). This change from highly intrusive conditionality to one of cooperation faced serious setbacks following nationwide riots in 2004, resulting in nineteen people dead and many Serb settlements being destroyed (Narten, 2009, p.266).

Other UN state-building operations had an influence on the Kosovan process. After violence resumed in East Timor in 2006, Annan acknowledged that the UN state-building mission had "been terminated prematurely" (Paris and Sisk, 2009, p.13). UNMIK took even greater control over the justice system in Kosovo allowing the special representative of the UN secretary general to designate sensitive trials to a special panel made up largely of international judges.

Apparent in the final stage of this project is the conflict between the UN's two objectives; firstly, creating functioning, secure, indigenous democratic institutions, and secondly, the "heavy footprint" approach to state-building necessary to create those institutions within the UN's designated timeframe. The UN's failure to stop genocide in Rwanda clearly informed both the discourse coming from UN policymakers, as well as their actions. Holkeri was quickly able to modify the UN's mission method to institution building because the approaches perceived conflicted with the stated aims of the mission and the UN's Pluralist foundations. This less conditional approach ended when the possibility of increased violence and unrest was exposed. This affirms a central tenant of DI theory: institutions serve both as structures constraining actors, but are also constructed and changed by those actors (Schmidt, 2008, p.314). Holkeri could change policies quickly because his approach was consistent with norms imbedded in the UN, but he saw those changes scaled back as serious threats emerged that had the potential of bringing about violent acts like those the UN failed to prepare for in Rwanda. The UNMIK approach to building Kosovan institutions were informed by both the imbedded norms in the organization, as well as those carried by policymakers responsible for those institutions.

A cornerstone to constructivist theory is the role previous ideas and discourses play on current norms and policy formations (Crawford, 2006, p.280). The logic behind greater intervention into Kosovo's domestic institutions can be traced through a chronological reading of UN reports concerning state-building throughout the 1990s. From 1992's "An Agenda for Peace" through the "Report of the Panel on United Nations Peace Operations" in 2000, norms were established that ultimately furthered the notion that a transitional administration must repair or create the foundations of the state that led to that state's instability (Ibid, p.277). Failure to deal with the underlying causes of conflict in former state-building exercises provided added credence to the UN's extensive mandate in Kosovo; this mandate allowed its leaders to increasingly intervene in the country's institutions when it believed the domestic situation was deteriorating.

Chapter 4:
Case Studies - U.S. State-building Afghanistan (2001-2010)/ Iraq (2003-2010)

Stage 1

Afghanistan: 2001-2002 – Iraq: 2003 – 2004

Following the 9/11 attacks, the United States overthrew

the Taliban in Afghanistan using a combination of aerial attacks,

special forces, precision-guided munitions, and indigenous allies

(Biddle, 2002, p.1). With superior military expertise and

technology, the United States quickly removed the Taliban from

power with few casualties to its armed forces. By December 5th,

2001 the Bonn Agreement was signed with Afghan leaders,

establishing a timetable for the reconstruction of the nation's

governmental institutions and security apparatus, using the

country's 1964 constitution as its foundation (USIP, 2004, p.3).

The agreement was not a peace accord: the Taliban never surrendered to American forces or the new Afghan transitional authority. The UN Security Council quickly authorized the International Security Assistance Force (ISAF), which deployed nearly 5,000 troops from nineteen countries to help establish security in Kabul by January 2002 (USIP, 2004, p.4). While the Afghan state-building project was predominantly U.S. lead, major portions of the project were given to coalition partners to manage (Ayub, 2008, p.652), and received initial support from the international community.

Unlike previous UN state-building projects in Bosnia, East Timor, and Kosovo, the United States adopted a "light footprint" approach to Afghanistan (Barfield, 2008, p.411). The level of assistance allocated to the Afghan project has been some of the lowest in any state-building project since the end of WWII (Jones et al, 2005, p.69). Additionally, most of the resources allocated to improving and creating justice and security institutions have been applied entirely to Kabul, leaving large parts of the state without any funding or resources (Ibid, p.69). This policy was surprising, especially since Afghanistan ranked near the bottom of the World Bank's list of countries experiencing weak rule of law, with confidence in the judiciary, government, and law enforcement at low levels (Jones et al, 2005, p.99). The reason for this tactical shift from the state-building lessons learned throughout the 1990s was not the product of ignorance; rather, the policymakers responsible for the Afghan state-building process had learned a separate set of lessons from the conflicts of the previous decade.

The Gulf War and the subsequent bombing campaigns in Yugoslavia altered American norms surrounding the use of force and the role of foreign powers in state-building exercises. During the first Gulf War, the United States had difficulty establishing a unified command structure to coordinate forces. One British officer stated that the European allies were less interested in a competent response, and more interested in "eroding American domination of NATO" (Lansford, 2002, pg.130). During the air campaign in Kosovo, many American military officers complained "of an excessive degree of political interference from other NATO allies in the daily aerial missions, even though the bulk of the aircraft used were American" (Ibid, pg.130).

Additionally, the U.S. also viewed the "No fly zones" established over Iraqi Kurdistan as successful representation of how superior American military strength could secure a region, allowing domestic actors the opportunity to rebuild (Wheeler, 2000, p.149). Feeling that multilateral agreements during military and state-building operations hindered the process, the U.S. endeavoured to streamline the command structure, granting itself sole responsibility and authority.

The theory that the United States could win wars quickly and decisively with few troops on the ground was popular in military and policy planning circles in the United States (Biddle, 1996, p.142). The United States initially alleged that it could defeat its enemy in Afghanistan with few troops using its superior airpower to target enemy locations from afar. The early stages of the war benefited coalition forces considerably, but this technological superiority became less successful as the enemy adapted to their circumstances. Al-Qaeda defences quickly began to use "systemic communications security, dispersal, camouflage discipline, use of cover and concealment, and exploitation of dummy fighting positions to draw fire and attention from their real positions" (Biddle, 2007, p.277). During Operation Anaconda in 2002, fewer than 50% of Al-Qaeda's defensive positions were discovered by aerial reconnaissance (Ibid, p.278). As enemy forces adapted to the American weapon systems, they revealed the limitations that technological superiority has on fighting concealed insurgencies (Ibid, p.280).

Unlike in Bosnia and Kosovo, the United States did not deploy international police forces in Afghanistan. This meant that the U.S. military or private contractors undertook the training of Afghan police. (Jones, 2005, p.73) At the Bonn Agreement, "Afghan and international stakeholders implicitly and explicitly accepted the logic that security and stability in the short term should be prioritized above accountability, peace and justice in the longer term" (Ayub, 2008, p.650). Indigenous Afghanis were considered acceptable statesmen if they were not Taliban and if they could stabilize the country (Ibid, p.650). Under the Bonn framework, ISAF provided security to the transitional administration until it could support itself, but it remained restricted to Kabul while warlords were given control of security throughout the rest of the country (Ibid, p.654). While the U.S.

military was present in the country, it operated under the auspices of Operation Enduring Freedom, which was dedicated to counterterrorism operations (Ibid, p.654). Tajiks, the ethnic group composing the Northern Alliance, immediately packed the government with their own supporters, "to the exclusion both of Pashtuns, the largest group in the population and minority Shi'a Hazaras" (Starr, 2004, p.2).

Terrorism was conceived as an existential threat to the United States and thus necessitated the rebuilding of the Afghani state to undermine this danger. Noah Feldman, a leading policymaker in the Bush administration, stated "there is no question that terrorism today is the greatest threat to the United States" (Feldman, 2005, p.8). Yet, once al-Qaeda and its supporters in the Taliban regime were defeated, the U.S. quickly averted attention away from Afghanistan and towards the U.S. effort to overthrow Saddam Hussein's regime in Iraq and introduce liberal democracy in the state.

The first phase of the Iraqi reconstruction was similar to what was seen in Afghanistan. A year before the United States invaded Iraq, Phebe Marr, a prominent Iraq scholar from the

National Defense University, told the Senate Foreign Relations

Committee that if the United States was going to exercise regime

change, "it must be prepared to put some troops on the ground,

advisers to help create new institutions, and above all, time and

effort in the future to see the project through to a satisfactory end"

(Fallows, 2004). The U.S. administration, though, opted for a

different policy in the initial stages of the project. Following what

was perceived to be a quick victory in Afghanistan, the U.S.

intended to transfer authority to domestic actors soon after the

overthrow of the regime, using as few troops and resources as

possible (Diamond, 2005, p.9). While major combat operations

ended soon after the invasion, the war had not technically ended

in surrender; meaning state-building operations would be

implemented during a period of active military conflict (Barakat,

2005, p.572; Edelstein, 2004, p.59).

The U.S. created a transitional administration called the

Coalition Provisional Authority (CPA) to oversee the rebuilding

of Iraq's institutions, and the eventual handover of state power to

indigenous authorities. The CPA's framework for rebuilding Iraqi

institutions was ambitious, setting out a grand reconstruction project it hoped to achieve within three months (CPA, 2003).

While the CPA stated that it would consult Iraqi Interim

Administrators and domestic leaders (CPA, 2003, p.5), the

authority rarely did so (Cordesman, 2010, p.17). The CPA

focused large portions of its resources on building infrastructure

related to constructing a functioning capitalist economy and left

major issues concerning education, elections, and domestic

institutions to local authorities (Cordesman, 2010, p.17). On

paper, the CPA had significant power to implement its very

ambitious goals. However, Paul Bremer and other American

authorities quickly learned that they had a "great responsibility

without commensurate power" (Ricks, 2006, p.205). The CPA

was understaffed, and it lacked the budget necessary to achieve

the authority's objectives. Managing over the semi-socialist state

that existed under Hussein's regime required a great deal of

micromanaging (Rathmell, 2008, p.1020). Additionally, the CPA

was given responsibility over all aspects of the state-building

process, except the state's security, which in the first year proved

to be the important sphere of responsibility (Ricks, 2006, p.205).

As the security situation quickly worsened, the U.S.

administration's plans found themselves at odds with their goals and assumptions (Tripp, 2007, p.277).

The Bush administration argued that economic liberalization would not only make Iraq wealthier but would provide security in the absence of the Hussein regime. This liberal economic policy "would negate the need for a large number of foreign troops, the deployment of large-scale US resources or an extended occupation" (Dodge, 2009, p. 265). Zalmay Khalilzad, the first U.S. ambassador to Iraq, stated that one of America's main state-building objectives was the reformation of the Iraqi economy to put the country "on the path to prosperity" (Etzioni, 2009, p.102). The UN Security Council subsequently passed Resolution 1483 (UNSCR 1483), requiring 95% of its fund into the Development Fund for Iraq (DFI) to pay for the country's rebuilding (SIGIR, 2009, p.80).

While the United States did prepare for the post-war state-building, they expected a situation that never materialized and were blinded by superior military prowess (Jones et al, 2006, p.111). Nearly all of the administrative structures of the state had collapsed by the time the Office for Reconstruction and

Humanitarian Assistance (ORHA) took over administrative duties in the country (Jones et al, 2005, p.111). By 2003, most of Iraq's internal security was policed through Ba'athist political organizations such as the Republican Guard and the Special Security Organization. As the initial stages of the war ended, many of these forces simply went underground. In May of 2003, the CPA disbanded the remaining Iraqi intelligence and security services, failing to recognize that these organizations played a more significant security role than the armed forces (Diamond, 2005, p.14).

Reconstructing the Iraqi Police Service (IPS) was one of the key tasks facing the transitional authority, but it received little attention from the CPA in its first year (Jones et al, 2005, p.118). Following de-Ba'athification, the CPA created the Iraqi Police Services (IPS), giving the new Iraqi police service the formal authority related to crime control and ordinance maintenance (Deflem and Sutphin, 2006, p.270). Coalition forces would investigate and pursue terrorist related criminal activity, but the burden of responsibility for general law enforcement was placed on the Iraqis. Many Iraqi police were retained from the previous regime, which produced negative results. In the weeks following the fall of Baghdad, U.S. forces began to integrate existing Iraqi police into their patrols, but this produced considerable outrage due to a feeling among the Iraqi populace that the remaining police officers were leftovers from the Ba'athist regime (Deflem and Sutphin, 2006, p.270) American police trainers complained that the Iraqi police were at best unreliable and often engaged in criminal or sectarian activities (Deflem and Sutphin, 2006, p.271). Additionally, international police were not present in Iraq, requiring the American military to carry out most of the training.

The norms that justified and formulated the first stage of the Iraqi state-building project can be observed in the statements made by policymakers in charge of the project at the time. After the first few months, Secretary of Defence Donald Rumsfeld, when discussing changes happening in the country, stated "If one looks back at Germany, at Japan, at Bosnia or Kosovo, and measures the progress that [has] taken place in this country in four or five months, it dwarfs any other experience that I'm aware of" (Ricks, 2006, p.242). Leading Bush administration officials habitually argued that the U.S. would be treated as liberators

(Cheney, 2003), and that the occupation would be short, with Iraqi oil reserves paying the financial cost (Gilmore, 2003). The U.S. government's faith in the power of liberal democracy informed their approach to democratic governance in both the Iraq and Afghani state-building operations, leading them to conclude that little in the way of assistance to the Iraqi and Afghani states would be necessary to create a functioning liberal democracy. American policymakers' insistence on democratic elections also exposed an ideological foundation to their policy; the Bush administration had accepted the basic premise of democratic peace theory, believing that democratic states were inherently more secure and peace prone (Owen, 2005, p.123).

Members of he U.S. administration also made allusions to the Solidarists origins of the Afghanistan and Iraqi state-building operations. Traditional references to U.S. national interests were rarely made by the administration, and instead focused on the need for the U.S. to spread liberal democratic regimes to "secure a peaceful world" (Kerton-Johnson, 2008, p.994). The Bush administration framed both wars in a moral framework that emphasised the need for pluralistic regimes, which were to the betterment of all "freedom-loving people around the world" (Kerton-Johnson, 2008, p.995). Additionally, U.S. policymakers conceived of their responsibility to the citizens in both states differently than did the human security precepts adopted by the UN. Coined the "War is hell" doctrine by Michael Walzer, the U.S. adopted a policy towards state-building that placed all responsibility for the loss of civilian life on enemy combatants (Wheeler, 2002, p.217). Donald Rumsfeld stated that the U.S. "did not start this war. So understand, responsibility for every single casualty in this war, whether they're innocent Afghans or innocent Americans, rests at the feet of the al-Qaeda and the Taliban" (Ibid, p.217). While the U.S. supported its state-building missions by arguing that its missions was for the good of Iraqi and Afghani citizens, and that the U.S. had a moral responsibility to intervene, their approach differed from recognized just-war theory, which emphasis "due care" in the protection of civilians (Ibid, p.215).

Placing reconstruction efforts in the hands of the military and believing that a speedy handover of power to domestic authorities would visibly result informed the first stage of these operations. DI theory states that institutional change "is dynamic and explainable across time through agents' ideas and discourse" (Schmidt, 2008, p.322), which we can observe in the U.S. military's approach to state-building. At the beginning of the project, policymakers believed that an army with precession-guided subsystems "has an overwhelming advantage over an army without it" (Perry, 1991, p.11). Most of the pre-war planning and responsibility during the first year of occupation was in the hands of the Department of Defence (DoD), which planning led to a primary disregard for civilian aspects and facilities during the occupation period (Cordesman, 2010, p.17). The DoD lacked the expertise, experience, and local knowledge in overseeing a large multi-agency civilian mission that the subsequent state-building operation required (Ricks, 2006, p.79). The normative rationale for why the DoD was given reigns over the operation was informed by previous U.S. operations in the post-Cold War world. State officials recognized the strength and capabilities of the military that had been achieved since the first Gulf War, as well as the problems working through multilateral organizations in previous state-building operations in the 1990s, leading them to deem the military as best suited for leading these state-building operations.

Additionally, the first stage of these state-building projects affirms the constructivist position that "ideas are shaped by the lived experience of groups…in distinct social locations" (Rueschemeyer, 2006, p.233). The U.S. military bureaucracy, with its own norms and discourse reflecting both its failures and triumphs, conceived of the state-building process in a way that emphasised its physical strengths. America's role as a unipolar power following the end of the Cold War sustained the Bush administration's assertion that the United States was the only entity capable of acting decisively to bring about a more democratic international society. These norms were not exclusively developed within the Bush administration however, and they are a product of the post-Cold War structure and international society (Kerton-Johnson, 2008, p.1000). Under Bill Clinton, the U.S. contributed to state-building operations around the world in an attempt to spread democracy and human rights (Mann, 2004, p.214). Madeleine Albright referred to the U.S. as the "indispensable nation," believing that America's role as the lone superpower bestowed upon it responsibilities and privileges other states did not have (Mann, 2004, p.214). The U.S. played a vital and crucial role in Bosnia and Kosovo, providing ample evidence that the United States could quickly and decisively bring an end to a conflict if it applied its power appropriately.

Stage 2

Afghanistan 2003-2005 – Iraq 2004-2006

The changes in policy between stage one and stage two appear small, but alterations in American norms concerning state-building began to adjust. The U.S. still intended to pass authority to domestic leaders as soon as possible, but the window in which that power could be passed was transformed; consequently, there followed the realization that an increasing level of commitment was going to be necessary to bring about even base level objectives. The American transitional authority recognized that its "small footprint" had failed to stabilize Iraq, usher in liberal democracy, and bring about a functioning liberal economy. Letting local leaders take control of the reconstruction process in Iraq and Afghanistan failed to produce results the American government found acceptable (SIGIR, 2009, p.240). Additionally, American rhetoric concerning democracy and human rights, as well as the norms imbedded in international society, forced the U.S. to adapt its policy to abide to the existing international normative framework.

Hamid Karzai was elected President in Afghanistan on November 4th, 2004, with his presidency appearing to be a major accomplishment in the reconstruction of the state. With a popular elected leader in charge of Afghanistan, the U.S. administration believed a quick handover of sovereignty would soon be achieved (Barfield, 2008, p.412). But the security situation had been deteriorating since 2003, and the Pentagon began to authorize a much greater involvement in the reconstruction of Afghanistan's institutions and civil apparatus by U.S. military forces. American soldiers began providing "humanitarian assistance and took on some road and school construction projects" (USIP, 2004, p.4). The DoD created a program to position "Provincial Reconstruction Teams" (PRTs) near major cities throughout the country (USIP, 2004, p.4). A similar conclusion was reached in Iraq. On the developmental end of the state-building process,

American authorities were faced with the realisation that Iraqi administrators would not be able to maintain new U.S. provided facilities. With their "outmoded technical skills, limited management capacity, and uneven access to spare parts and supplies," indigenous authorities were not prepared to take control of these key industries, forcing the U.S. to rethink their timetable for handing over control (SIGIR, 2009, p.232).

The scattergun approach to reconstruction used in the first stage appeared to have failed. The U.S. Army Corp of Engineers Project and Contracting Office responsible for over $18.4 billion in reconstruction aid produced a long list of projects it intended to undertake (Etzioni, 2009, p.110). From the renovation of court houses, to the building of health facilities and schools, the U.S. government still maintained that its bold plans for rebuilding Iraq were underway, even though most of these projects were never completed (Etzioni, 2009, p.110). Many of the reconstruction endeavours were given to domestic authorities around the country, with little to no oversight into whether the project was underway or if it was necessary (Etzoni, 2009, p.111). In some cities, local leaders were not consulted on what types of projects and funding were necessary in their regions (Pillai, 2009, p.35). Reconstruction efforts also began to shift away from large scale, high profile projects to more equitable development focused on Iraqi citizens (Brown, 2005, p.769). There was recognition that the early stages of planning did not take focus on human security, neglecting areas with poor basic infrastructure (Brown, 2005, p.768), which then contributed to security and political problems.

There were also signs that the U.S. was backing away from its reconstruction agenda to focus more attention on the countries security. By September of 2005, U.S. officials shifted $5.59 billion, almost a third of reconstruction appropriations, to support security-related sectors (SIGIR, 2009, p.329). Prior to this, the U.S. began to provide more resources to the State Department to improve civilian reconstruction efforts and to reverse budget shortfalls that resulted in the State Department closing most of its CPA provincial officers (Ibid, p.239). A small amount of resources was spent on the Iraq Relief and Reconstruction Fund (IRRF) 1 and IRRF 2 democracy projects, which aimed to teach Iraqi administrators how to work in a democratic society. These projects received little funding however, and their success is hard to measure (Ibid, p.238).

Additionally, senior military commanders in Iraq continued to argue that the best approach was a limited one, forcing Iraqis to deal with their own reconstruction and security efforts. General John Abizaid, commander of U.S. Central Command since mid-2003, and George Casey, commander of Multi-National Forces-Iraq since 2004, argued that a visible presence throughout the country would only produce more resistance to the transitional authority and that the U.S. should continue its "light footprint" approach (Keane and Kagan, 2007, p.5).

While superior weapon systems allowed the U.S. to achieve military dominance in the early stages of the conflict, the assuredness that these capabilities would maintain security within the state throughout the state-building process was strained. In Afghanistan, the only physical presence throughout large parts of the country was allied warlords, often benefiting some actors in the country at the expense of others, and often to the detriment to the U.S. state-building operation (Day and Freeman, 2003, p.302). Evidence emerged that warlords allied with the U.S. were using their influence to bring American military attacks on rival leaders who had no connection to al-Qaeda or the Taliban, undermining national reconstruction efforts (Day and Freeman, 2003, p.302). On the world stage, the American military was unrivalled physically and technologically, yet this strength was "irrelevant for the achievement of the war's aims," both in establishing a democratic government in Iraq and Afghanistan and in "creating a new order in the Middle East" (Press-Barnathan, 2004, p.204).

The Bush administration's rhetoric on the justification for American involvement in both states demonstrates how norms and discourse restrict an actor's policy options. In Bush's 2004 State of the Union address, he stated that "America is a nation with a mission, and that mission comes from our most basic beliefs. We have no desire to dominate, no ambitions of empire" (Bush, 2004). While the U.S. administration's core case for both wars was security related, "American policy-makers would come to embrace the language and rhetoric of a humanitarian cause" (Ayub, 2008, p.647). In the months leading up to the Iraqi invasion, Bush stated that he had "faith in the transformative power of freedom and belief that people, if just given a chance, will choose free societies" (Woodward, 2008, p. 433). There were domestic political reasons for this rhetorical focus on democracy promotion, as the Bush administration faced a contested re-election campaign. Yet, this discourse also narrowed the policy options available to the U.S. and to its transitional administrations in Iraq and Afghanistan. Arguing that democracy and stability must be achieved in both states, the administration placed these aims in a privileged position above material state interests (Rueschemeyer, 2006, p.246). This "explicit commitment" to a norm reaffirms its centrality in guiding policy (Price, 2006, p.254), having "productive power" over the possible policies connected to state-building (Price, 2006, p.256). By furthering these norms in the public sphere, the American administration was enforcing a regulative effect on American options in Iraq and Afghanistan, specifying standards of appropriate behaviour (Katzenstein, 1996, p.5). Even if the administration had championed democracy promotion for selfish domestic reasons, reiterating those norms as descriptive principles contributed to making them important considerations in devising policy (Russett 1993, p.136).

Stage 3

Afghanistan 2006-2010 – Iraq 2007-2010

Significant changes in policy are observed in the third stage of both of these state-building projects. These changes are due to two factors: firstly, to the perceived success of the counterinsurgency "Surge" strategy spearheaded in Iraq by General David Petraeus; and secondly, to the effect this had on American norms regarding state-building. The limited approach used in the previous stages "failed to empower" Afghan and Iraqi institutions and was unable to ensure their reliability in rebuilding either state (Ayub, 2008, p.653). What then developed was a transition away from the light footprint approach to a more intensive and engaged state-building policy.

In late 2006, as violence in Iraq hit record levels and fears of civil war were high, the Bush administration went about radically rethinking and restructuring its state-building methods. John Keane and Frederick Kagan, the architects of the American state-building strategy now called "the Surge," argued that the U.S. must rethink its basic approach to reconstructing Iraq. In their influential "Choosing Victory: A Plan for Success in Iraq,"

Kagan argued that "securing the population has never been the primary mission of the U.S. military effort in Iraq, and now it must become the first priority" (Keane and Kagan, 2007, p.1), and that reconstruction efforts should be intrinsically linked to establishing and maintaining security (Keane and Kagan, 2007, p.2).

The Surge strategy increased the number of American troops in Iraq and made further changes to the American approach (see Figure 4). The U.S. began to apply the existing troops and resources in a way that can be described as a "conceptual revolution," adapting to previous mistakes in Iraq, as well as applying state-building lessons from recent UN missions (ICG, 2008, p.i). The most significant change in policy was the military's focus on protecting civilians. Unlike previous stages of the Iraqi state-building process, military personnel did not live and work in the communities they were trying to protect; instead, the personnel regulated its presence to military establishments, allowing them only to interact with Iraqi populace while on patrol (West, 2009, p.4). This strategy moved soldiers into neighbourhoods experiencing ethnic strife or was controlled by terrorists and militias, putting them at a much greater danger of attack (Ibid, p.4). This meant that American soldiers would take on riskier missions, placing them in troubled neighbourhoods for prolonged periods. Facets of Walzer's Just-War theory clearly informed this new approach. Walzer recognized that "if saving civilian lives means risking soldier's lives, the risk must be accepted" (Walzer, 1978, p.156). Originally opposed to this outlook, the U.S. eventually chose to adopt the approach by this stage of its state-building process. More than simply providing physical security, military personnel were "expected to be nation builders as well as warriors rebuilding infrastructure and basic services" (DoA, 2006). The role of U.S. military personnel in these missions gradually made positive changes in the country's security, significantly dropping the level of violence (SIGIR, 2009, p.295). Additionally, by protecting Iraqi citizens who were opposed to terrorist or insurgent groups attacking the Iraqi government and U.S. troops, the new civilian-focused strategy provided an opening to Sunni organizations to work with the Iraqi federal government and to remove belligerents from their communities (Koloski and Kolasheski, 2009, p.44).

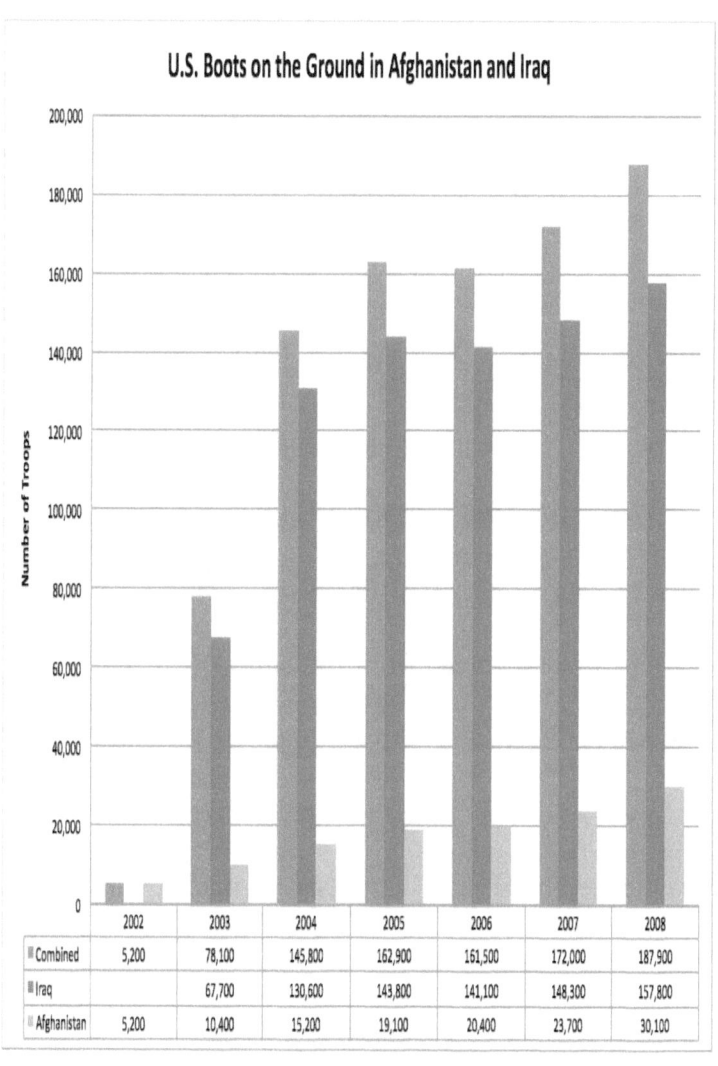

	2002	2003	2004	2005	2006	2007	2008
Combined	5,200	78,100	145,800	162,900	161,500	172,000	187,900
Iraq		67,700	130,600	143,800	141,100	148,300	157,800
Afghanistan	5,200	10,400	15,200	19,100	20,400	23,700	30,100

(Figure 4) (Source: Belasco, 2009, DoD 2002-2008)

The USAID's Community Stabilization Program was increased and began to focus on more modest infrastructure products in Iraqi neighbourhoods that would employ low skilled workers in those communities (SIGIR, 2009, p.308). The diplomatic and economic strategy employed was altered; until this point, most economic projects were working independently of each other and of the American security strategy. In the planning stages of the war, USAID Administrator Andrew Natsios, the highest-ranking Administration official to have both development and combat experience, was not invited to preparation meetings until the war began (SIGIR, 2009, p.325). By placing the project almost solely in the hands of military officials, U.S. policy planners devised a strategy divorced from strategies employed by the UN in Kosovo. Whereas various aspects of the state-building process in Kosovo were given to specialised groups familiar with one facet of the practice, the U.S. military was responsible for major parts of the process in Iraq.

Ryan Crocker became U.S. Ambassador to Iraq, and he agreed with General Petraeus that bureaucrats working on development and economic matters had to work closer with the military; this partnership allowed the U.S. to use both military coercion as well as "political negotiation and economic aid" to bring warring parties towards reconciliation (SIGIR, 2009, p.298). Petraeus argued that institutions of America's state-building apparatus outside the DoD had been under-funded, and guaranteeing them adequate resources was "of enormous importance" (SIGIR, 2009, p.300). Members of the PRT staff were embedded with each brigade, providing these units with a dedicated staff of development experts (SIGIR, 2009, p.300). A similar conclusion was made in Afghanistan, with policymakers recognizing that "an incomplete or misguided political analysis" had been used that saw the project in overly military terms (Ayub, 2008, p.648).

This combination of military ability and reconstruction efforts also became the dominate approach in Afghanistan. Building the Afghan National Security Forces (ANSF) had been a priority for the American government, but a suitable force had yet to materialize. In 2006-2007, the ANSF began to have meaningful objectives and benchmarks and began to receive significant ISAF and US aid in developing its "force quantity" (Cordesman,

2010,p.ii). In March of 2009, the U.S released its new strategy on Afghanistan. The document stated that the U.S. would integrate its civilian-military counterinsurgency strategy, improve local governance, counter corruption, and develop more self-reliant Afghan security forces (U.S. Gov, 2009, p.1). The plan looked similar to the Surge strategy employed in Iraq and demonstrated that the U.S. was fundamentally changing its strategy in Afghanistan to meet new objectives and concerns (Jones, 2009, p.2). This "bottom-up" strategy recognized that the security of the country's inhabitants was at the forefront of the counterinsurgency strategy and of the success of the state-building operation (Jones, 2009, p.7).

There is a significant change in norms presented in stage three. Etzioni argues that a low level of social order and security often produces "strong anti-democratic tendencies" (Etzioni, 2007, p.157). For the liberal democratic ideals to become internalised modes of operation, the U.S. would need to stabilize each country before loftier objectives could be achieved. Additionally, aspects of the UN's human security model, such as food and individual citizen security, were incorporated into the military and civilian strategies to achieve these ends. Upon removing violent domestic elements from a neighbourhood, USACE moved in to restore water, electrical, and sanitation services (SIGIR, 2009, p.297). Without basic security, reconstruction efforts could not be carried out, but a broader understanding of what constituted a secure society was necessary to repair equally destructive social issues (SIGIR, 2009, p.331). As the UNDP argued, "A threat to one element of human security is likely to travel-like an angry typhoon – to all forms of human security" (UNDP, 2004, p.33).

The changes in policy between stage one and three represents both the regulative and constitutive effect that norms have had on U.S. policy. As noted previously, regulative effects "specify standards of proper behaviour" (Katzenstein, 1996, p.5). The U.S. accepted a greater commitment in Iraq and Afghanistan because its standing on the international stage would be damaged by not abiding the accepted rules of conduct. Moreover, as these norms developed, they had constitutive effects on policymakers responsible for these operations. "The Surge" redefines the role of the American soldier, fundamentally connecting their efforts to larger reconstruction efforts. According to Discursive Institutionalism, changes in America's approach can be attributed "through constructive discourse about ideas" within institutions responsible for these operations (Schmidt, 2008, p.316). Rather than being locked-in to an institution's normative paradigm, individuals can debate and reason within an organization, changing the structures they use (Schmidt, 2008, p.316). Petraeus, Kagan, and Keane contested the assumed role and policy options available to the U.S. in its state-building mission, altering how these institutions approached the process.

One also observes how the shape of an institution relies heavily on the influence of "organizational leadership" as they shape the goals "actually pursued by the organization and its followers" (Rueschemeyer, 2006, p.244). Petraeus was able to advance his policy by understanding the institutional structure he was operating within. Before Petraeus was given control, "there often seemed to be dozens of wars going on, with every brigade commander trying to figure out the strategic goals of a campaign. Before Petraeus arrived, the top priority for U.S. forces was getting out" (Ricks, 2010). Upon taking control of the mission, he reaffirmed a central mission and objective across the various U.S. government agencies, directing them to work towards an achievable goal with the protection of Iraqi civilians as its central objective (Ricks, 2010).

Wendts and Buzan's model explaining internalisation of norms provides insight into how a society's rules are regulated (Wendt, 1999, p.247-254). A society's norms are followed due to coercion, calculation, or belief on the part of that society's citizens (Buzan, 2004, p.132-133). Key policymakers in the U.S. administration believed liberal market principles would have a significant social imprint on Iraqi citizens, compelling them to build a new society on basic capitalist principles and rely less on the state (Yousif, 2006, p.501).By providing liberal social structures, the U.S. and its transitional administration in Iraq believed a quick transformation of Iraq's economy would yield success for other aspects of their state-building. Liberal ideals influenced the Bush administration early in the process by conceiving of individuals as the actors being saved in these interventions (Dodge, 2009, p.262), but the liberal belief in the constitutive power of a market economy also provided the foundation to the early stages of state-building. Liberalism believes that a market enforces within individuals a set of virtues such as caution, diligence, regularity and self-control (Hindess, 2002, p. 135). While liberal markets and societies may produce such an effect within individuals, a liberal society requires more than the economic foundation of capitalism to exist. Reforming a countries' economic sector proved more difficult (Yousif, 2006, p.502), and with basic services and security not provided for, the belief in the power of liberal economic policies to bring swift change was diminished. By accepting the more intrusive Surge strategy, the U.S. drifted from their principled position that belief in and of itself could achieve their state-building aims after the initial military invasion.

On this internalisation scale, U.S. policy moved further from the belief realm into calculation and coercion. By placing an increased number of troops in Iraqi communities experiencing security problems, the American military provided the security required to coerce insurgents by confronting them repeatedly in their own territory; they also provided the necessary security to sway community leaders towards opposing terrorist organizations

72

in their areas. Prior to this, community leaders calculated that it was best to work with terrorist and insurgents fighting American soldiers and the Iraqi government. Once their basic safety was improved by increased patrols and counterinsurgency tactics, many local leaders calculated that their interests were better met by removing terrorist groups from their communities (ICG, 2008, p.22).

As with all state-building cases, but specifically those with overt Solidarists elements, it is not simply a matter of what values are shared among a community; rather it is a matter of how and why those norms are shared (Buzan, 2008, p.153). Conrad Crane of the Army War College argued that history shows that successful occupations are best executed by demonstrating superior military technology, and then by drawing down the number of troops quickly, to minimize the potential for an uprising, an idea that was popular with policymaking institutions responsible for these American state-building projects (Fallows, 2004). As greater involvement in Iraqi and Afghani institutions was instigated, U.S. policy moved from its initial faith in the power of their ideas to reconstruct these states. The basic premise of the "Surge" strategy in Iraq is a testament to this; by increasing

the number of troops active in Iraqi communities and their scope

of operation, the U.S. forced indigenous actors in troubled

communities to calculate the benefit of fighting the Iraqi

government versus the risk of cooperating with the new regime.

In the first few months of the conflict, many policy planners

simply assumed these domestic actors would side with the U.S.

and the new Iraqi government. Instead, U.S. policy planners

found that portions of the state were not willing to work within

their desired framework. The U.S. would need to provide Iraqi

citizens with basic security, of the technical and human variety, if

the U.S. wanted the population to support the new regime over

competing organizations and ideals.

Chapter 5:
Constructed Norms or Material Advantage?

In both American state-building cases, we see that what was initially conceived as a modest state-building operation, eventually "ballooned into an expansive and expensive" program (SIGIR, 2009, p.331). American transitional administrations attempted to stabilize and liberalize Iraq and Afghanistan by empowering local authorities to spearhead the reconstruction process and stabilize their states. As this approach failed to produce acceptable results, policymakers responsible for these operations recognized that adequate security and functioning government institutions "cannot be established without promoting accountability and the rule of law" (Ayub, 2008, p.656). This resulted in a more interventionist policy that saw a greater number of troops active in these states, as well as a renewed focus on providing basic tenets of human security.

Materialist theorists would argue that the change in American policy throughout the course of these wars has little to do with socially constructed norms and more to do with tangible, measurable interests. I do not dispute that material benefits (both in resources and power in the international system) influence the policy making process. However, purely materialist explanations cannot explain the changes in American policy towards a more interventionist state-building mode of operation throughout the course of the project. Kenneth Waltz argued that a theory is meant to explain only part of reality and that the isolation of a small number of factors on one level of a system is necessary to devise an adequate theoretical premise (Waltz, 1990, p.7,10). To Waltz and other neorealists, the structure of the international system affects the way states behave and the outcomes they produce (Waltz, 1990, p.37). Rather than examining the motivations behind policymakers' decisions, he asserts that "the world must be drastically simplified; subtleties must be rudely pushed aside, and reality must be grossly distorted," rejecting and "belittling" normative power as a legitimate rationalization for action (Waltz, 1990, p.27; Etzioni, 2005b, p. 1663). States are all guided by similar motivations in devising their foreign policies, which "objectively limits the kinds of choices available to states and their leaders" (Payne, 2007, p.504).

While Waltz is surely correct to argue that the structure of the international system is an important factor in how states behave, his argument is not the only variable that needs to be examined. A more holistic approach must be applied. As previously noted, the U.S. and the UN had a number of policy options with which to advance throughout the duration of their state-building exercises. Only by examining the norms and perceptions apparent in the decision-making process can we discern why one option was advanced over another. The U.S. could have maintained the "small footprint" approach to Afghanistan and Iraq if its goal was simply to thwart terrorist groups from attacking the United States.

Historically, political leaders often claim that their actions are for the good of all people but hide generally selfish intentions. Hans Morgenthau alleged that statesmen and policymakers must pay tribute to ethical standards for the "realization of his political goal" (Morgenthau, 1945, p.5). While examples of this are numerous throughout history (Morgenthau, 1948, p.81), brushing aside norms and perceptions, thereby rendering them unimportant in understanding state action misconstrues the power that discourse has in constituting and regulating norms related to action (Katzenstein, 1996, p.5). If it was simply a cost versus benefit analysis, increased involvement in these projects, costing more blood and treasure, is a far more expensive approach than the minimal options available. As Barnett Rubin argued, the U.S. could have achieved its aims of removing terrorists from Afghanistan and Iraq with cheaper and easier methods (Rubin, 2004, p.167). Some scholars and policymakers argue that the U.S. should accept that ethnic and cultural divisions were insurmountable, that more modest approaches should be implemented focusing on core, measurable, and material interests rather than the state-building operations currently devised (Leverett, 2005). Even if states act out of ulterior materialist concerns, they are still bound to uphold humanitarian norms related to the state-building process in subsequent actions if they wish to maintain their standing in the international community

(Wheeler, 2000, p.288). Yet, the loftier rhetoric surrounding democracy promotion requires a state-building policy that will realize those aims.

Employing Waltz's version of neorealism to explain state-building operations is problematic for a number of reasons. Waltz recognized that a theory needed to lack complexity if it was to be useable, and thus he constructed a model to simply explicate the international systemic structure (Waltz, 1990, p.31). It was not intended to explain actions by units on other levels or systems. Yet, here lies a conflict within neorealism's structural model; by arguing that the units composing a state or any decision-making body are not relevant to the very character of the institution inherently contradicts the normative changes demonstrated in the previous case studies. The manner in which policymakers, as well as the states and organizations they lead, conceive of norms and rules in turn produces different policies on the international stage. The alternatives to the chosen policies used in Kosovo, Afghanistan, and Iraq were numerous (Leverett, 2007). Many of those alternatives would have been cheaper for the foreign transitional authority and arguably would have been more in touch with those organizations' material interests. Yet, these organizations opted to further policies that reflected norms surrounding the decision making body that had developed in the end of the Cold War.

The Iraq Study Group produced a report in 2006 that offered alternatives to "the Surge" strategy eventually undertaken by the U.S. The report recommended that the number of American troops be significantly lowered and that the number of imbedded soldiers in Iraqi Army units be increased (2006, p.48). It implicitly argued that state-building operations should predominately be in the hands of Iraqis, and that it was ultimately the responsibility of the Iraqi people to establish order (2006, p.42). Claude Salhani of the United Press International stated that the report offered to the American administration an "honorable exit strategy from the Iraq quagmire" (Salhani, 2006), with prominent American politicians agreeing that the report offered a path towards a drawdown in support from Iraq (Sweet, 2006).

Debates within the military over the correct approach to state-building in Iraq and Afghanistan demonstrate the level of contention within these policymaking circles and reveal how a single approach is not a forgone conclusion. In 2006, Jack Keane, then working on the Defence Policy Review Board, made the case for a much greater military and financial commitment to Iraq, a care that Donald Rumsfeld rejected (Barnes, 2008). Retired generals Wayne Downing and Barry McCaffrey, as well as CENTCOM commander General John Abizaid, opposed the Surge strategy and were heavily involved in the decision-making process, arguing for a lighter approach (Ibid). President Bush was presented with more than one serious policy option before deciding on the Surge. From continuing the existing strategy, to significantly increasing the level of involvement in the process, the administration also considered abandoning both strategies. Such a policy would have moved all American personnel to the borders of the country, "let[ting] [Iraqis] fight it out" while making sure the violence did not spread beyond the state's borders (Barnes, 2008). Yet even with top military commanders opposed to the Surge, and with the increased level of resources it would entail, the U.S. opted for the strategy.

In November of 2009, U.S. ambassador to Afghanistan and retired Army lieutenant general Karl Eikenberry challenged the developing strategy in Afghanistan. He argued that the U.S. underestimated "the risks of [the] expansion of our mission" and that increased involvement would further their belief amongst some in the Afghan population that the U.S. only "covet[s] their territory for a never-ending war on terror" (Eikenberry, 2009, p.1-2). Apparently, Eikenberry's position failed to influence key policymakers, who have opted for a Surge strategy that reflects a change in norms and the policy options following its implementation in Iraq (Norton-Taylor, 2010).

By disregarding international norms in entering Iraq without UN approval, U.S. policymakers carried out a policy focusing on structural power at the systemic level, undermining norms established since the end of the Cold War (Press-Barnathan, 2004, p.207). The United States sought to overthrow the Iraqi regime, and when the key norm producing international institution rejected them (the UN), they chose to ignore the institution and act unilaterally. The initial stages of the state-building projects also appear to support neorealist precepts (Press-Barnathan, 2004, p.2007). The U.S. believed it could ignore international social norms by succeeding in establishing liberal democracies quickly in both states, as a swift and victorious operation would provide the unilateral missions legitimacy in retrospection (Edelstein, 2004, p.71). However, the increased commitment made by the American government to the transitional administrations demonstrates how norms influence policy. This is a challenge to the neorealist precept that power is understood as physical capabilities (Wendt, 1999, p.92), as non-measurable normative standards have the ability to shape and transform the behaviour of states. The United States is not forced to follow these international norms (as demonstrated by its willingness to invade Iraq without UN Security Council approval) but was constrained in its actions in later stages of the state-building process due to its willingness to follow international standards of action.

Cristoph Wilcke argued that the Bush administration had "dug its own policy grave" by proclaiming so vociferously that a democratic transformation of Iraq and Afghanistan was necessary to completing the U.S. mission in both states (Wilcke, 2004, p.4). Following this line of reasoning, the U.S. would be forced to commit itself to a state-building approach that was not in its best interests, but was merely "saving face" by furthering the current policy (Paul, 2007). Colin Powell argued that by invading Iraq, the U.S. had an obligation to then fix the state, something glibly referred to as the "Pottery Barn rule" (Haddick, 2010). All of these arguments affirm the power of ideas and norms in the state-building process. All three statements intrinsically recognize that other policy options are available to the U.S. and its transitional administrations in Iraq and Afghanistan. Yet as a result of the discourse expressed by the Bush administration, the desire not to be seen as irresponsible or inconsistent within the international society, and the imbedded normative belief that the U.S. has a moral responsibility to help rebuild a state following a military intervention it spearheaded, the U.S. committed itself to a more devoted approach to its state-building endeavours in Iraq and Afghanistan.

Waltz's theory works on the premise that interests are material in nature rather than representations of a specific idea (Wendt, 1999, p.98). Arguing that behaviour is defined solely by material interest presents a problem with the causal approach to understanding conduct begins to emerge. By focusing primarily on why "X" produced an independently existing "Y," it avoids the very nature of what constitutes "X" and "Y" to begin with (Wendt, 1999, p.83). Without understanding how the international society or an institution is built, we cannot comprehend how certain policies are accepted and varying alternatives, are not accepted (Wendt, 1999, p.87). Actors are dependent on the ideas and structures that they are part of and that they constitute (Ibid, p.88).

As noted in the case studies, alternative policies were offered by leading policymakers in the institutions responsible for these operations. Top generals and diplomats challenged the "heavy footprint" approach developed by stage 3, arguing that less involvement in reconstruction efforts furthered American interests. These leading policymakers failed to realize their policy recommendations, even in cases where they were associated to the material interests connected to the wars. In this sense, we see that norms have changed how states and international bodies approach these operations. There is an implication that something is owed to the people in these states and that a state's standing in the international community will be damaged by not fulfilling those requirements. Hedley Bull stated that limitations on the use of violence has been one of the defining characteristics of the international society (Bull, 1977, p.10-15), something American policymakers surely supposed based on its desire to see its military actions as legitimate in the eyes of the international community (BBC, 2010).

Yet, many neorealists building on Waltz's structural theory to explain state action argue that the debate surrounding intervention and state-building is important in the domestic sphere – something inconsistent with a systemic theory (Payne, 2007, p.504). John Mearsheimer, a leading academic neorealist, argued that during the 2002 congressional debate concerning Iraq, the Bush administration "basically steamrollered their way on this, and the price is we won't have the debate we should" (Westphal and James, 2002, p.A1). The Coalition for a Realistic Foreign Policy, an organization made up of neorealist politicians and scholars, called for a "broad and public debate" concerning American foreign policy (Payne, 2007, p.504). Implicit in these statements is the importance of debate and discourse in devising and applying a policy. Persuading policymakers and citizens is thus a necessary endeavour to instigating their policy precepts. These neorealists recognize that how a public or institutional debate occurs is significant, a position much closer to constructivist theories like DI. Rather than states and institutions being locked into path-dependent approaches, agents maintain or change intuitions using their "background ideational abilities" (Schmidt, 2008, p.314) Institutions are taken as a given, insofar as they act and articulate positions but also contingent upon various inputs that result from its agent's thoughts, words, and actions (Ibid, p.314). These prominent neorealists, while maintaining the authority of the international system above all other levels, promote an approach on discourse inconsistent with systemic theorizing. Just as the "evolving normative background and social structure" of the international society contributed to the increased level of intervention in the affairs of other states (Alkopher, 2007, p.26), so too did the normative framework actors devise policy within influence how an actor behaves, but inclined the standards pertaining to how they *should* perform (Payne, 2007, p.510).

The increasing scope of the American state-building missions also supports a normative explanation of policymaking.

The initial reason for entering Afghanistan, to destroy al-Qaeda and capture individuals responsible for the 9/11 terrorist attack, appeared to no longer be the reason for maintaining the war by the beginning of stage 3. Al-Qaeda was a spent force, with most of its leaders hiding in Pakistan (Jenkins, 2009). In July of 2010, CIA director Leon Panetta asserted that there were no more than 100 al-Qaeda operatives in Afghanistan (Sanger, 2010). Yet, the United States is now committing more resources than at any point in the state-building process (see Figure 4). By examining the normative changes, both external and internal to an institution, constructivist explanations for policy transformation emerge as more accurate than specific structural rationalizations.

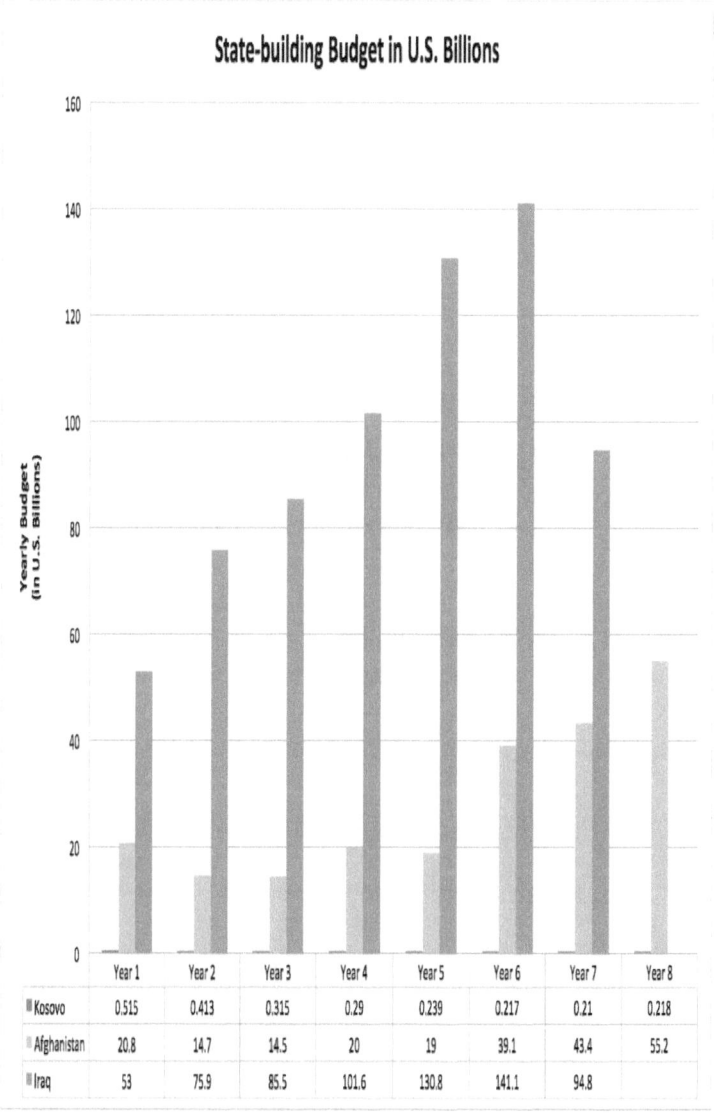

State-building Budget in U.S. Billions

	Year 1	Year 2	Year 3	Year 4	Year 5	Year 6	Year 7	Year 8
Kosovo	0.515	0.413	0.315	0.29	0.239	0.217	0.21	0.218
Afghanistan	20.8	14.7	14.5	20	19	39.1	43.4	55.2
Iraq	53	75.9	85.5	101.6	130.8	141.1	94.8	

(Figure 4) (Source: Belasco, 2009, IISS mutiple years)

Chapter 6:
Conclusion

As constructivists argue, ideas matter (Rueschemeyer, 2006, p.248; Schmidt, 2008, p.316; Wendt, 1999, p.370). Ideas shape the ways actors think within a specific institution and the norms that govern action among states in the international society. Understanding how and why these norms change, and the resulting effect they have on policy, requires a multilevel approach that a materialist structural theory cannot supply. As demonstrated in the state-building case studies examined in this dissertation, norms have both a regulative and constitutive effect on how actors perform. Yet, actors are not locked into a specific normative framework imbedded in an institution of the international society: they have the capacity to modify the ideas that lead to a definite set of policy prescriptions.

The changes in norms relating to the relations between states from reciprocal interaction following the Second World War, to conditional in the post-Cold War reveal how the rules that oversee action on the world stage can change. DI builds on this constructivist understanding of change by including individual agency within a normative institutional framework. Applying DI's logic to the importance of ideas in a society or an institution provides an explanation into how individual ideas and perceptions can alter an institution's course or normative foundation.

The policymakers responsible for the early stages of the war and state-building operations in Iraq and Afghanistan planned the mission from a militarized mindset that placed great importance on physical capabilities (Monten, 2005, p.151). The relative ease with which the U.S. and its allies expelled Iraq from Kuwait in 1990 and Serbia from Kosovo in 1999 reinforced the perception that overwhelming military strength could replace the resources, troops, and reconstruction tools to maintain security following hostilities. Planners in the Bush administrations built on these norms and maintained that indigenous actors in both states would quickly adopt liberal democratic ideals with little assistance from a foreign transitional authority. Framed within the "War on Terror" narrative, policymakers originally placed fighting terrorist organizations above securing the stability in both states. All of these frameworks contained imbedded norms and rules that produced the policy prescriptions within the first stage. As these approaches failed to achieve their desired aims, individuals within the leading policymaking institutions challenged the imbedded logic and discourse within these organizations, shifting the policies carried out in later stages.

Policymakers had options available to them outside of the chosen paths they adopted, informed by normative structures and perceptions on multiple systemic levels, so why did they decide to further their state-building operations in the manner they did? I have argued that ideas and norms are at the heart of a specific policy and institution. As demonstrated in this paper, institutions are maintained not through arbitrary linkages but through a mutually constitutive process that shapes both an actor's decision making as well as the very character of the institution (Schmidt, 2008, p.315). States and institutions are not locked into a specific policy; power and materialist concerns matter, but they are only a part of why actors behave as they do. Interests are ideas; the benefits of following accepted internationally, domestic, and institutionally norms forces actors to conceive of action in ways that are removed from a purely materialist perspective.

Bibliography

Abdela, Lesley. (2003). "Kosovo: Missed Opportunities, Lessons for the Future." *Development in Practice*, Vol. 13, No. 2/3, pp. 208-216.

Alkopher, Tal Dingott. (2007). "The Role of Rights in the Social Construction of Wars: From the Crusades to Humanitarian Interventions." *Millennium*, Vol. 36, No. 1, pp.1-27.

Allen, Michael. (2006). "Beyond Neo-conservatism." Democratiya.

Ayub, Fatima and Kouvo, Sari. (2008). "Righting the course? Humanitarian intervention, the war on terror and the future of Afghanistan." *International Affairs*, Vol. 84, No. 4, pp. 641-657.

Annan, Kofi. (1999b). *Preventing War and Disaster: A Growing Global Challenge*. UN Annual Report on the Works of the Organization, New York.

Annan, Kofi. (1999) "Two Concepts of Sovereignty." *The Economist*, September 18th. Available at: http://www.un.org/News/ossg/sg/stories/articleFull.asp?TID=33& Type=Article

Bain, William. (2003). "The Political Theory of Trusteeship and the Twilight of International Equality." *International Relations*, Vol. 17, No. 1, pp. 59-77.

Barakat, Sultan. (2005). "Post-Saddam Iraq: Deconstructing a Regime. Reconstructing a Nation." *Third World Quarterly*, Vol. 26, No. 4/5. pp. 571-581.

Barfield, Thomas. (2008). "The Roots of Failure in Afghanistan." *Current History*, Vol. 107, Is. 713, pp. 410-417.

Barnes, Fred. (2008). "How Bush Decided on the Surge." *The Weekly Standard*, Vol. 13, No. 20. Available at: http://www.weeklystandard.com/Content/Public/Articles/000/000/014/658dwgrn.asp

BBC. (2010). "US chief Petraeus vows to protect Afghan civilians." BBC World News, July 1st. Available at: http://news.bbc.co.uk/1/hi/world/south_asia/10472555.stm

Belasco, Amy. (2009). "The Cost of Iraq, Afghanistan, and Other Global War on Terror Operations Since 9/11." Congressional Research Service, September 28th.

Biddle, Stephen. (1996). Victory Misunderstood: What the Gulf War Tells Us about the Future of Conflict." *International Security*, Vol. 21, No. 2, pp. 139-179.

Biddle, Stephen. (2002). *Afghanistan and the Future of Warfare: Implications for Army and Defense Policy*. U.S. Army War College, Strategic Studies Institute, Department of Defence.

Biddle, Stephen. (2007). Iraq, Afghanistan, and American Military Transformation. In: Baylis, John and Wirtz, James and Gray, Colin and Cohen, Eliot *Strategy in the Contemporary World*. New York, NY: Oxford University Press. pp. 274-294.

Brown, Richard. (2005). "Reconstructing Infrastructure in Iraq: End to a Means or Means to an End?" *Third World Quarterly*, Vol. 26, No. 4/5, pp. 759-775.

Bull, Hedley. (1977). *The Anarchical Society*. London: Macmillan Press LTD.

Buzan, Barry (2004). *From International to World Society? English School Theory and the Social Structure of Globalisation.* Cambridge: Cambridge University Press.

Caplan, Richard (2005). *International Governance of War-Torn Territories: Rule and Reconstruction.* Oxford: Oxford University Press.

Cheney, Dick. (2003). Interview with Vice-President Dick Cheney, NBC, "Meet the Press," Transcript for March 16, 2003. Available at:
http://www.mtholyoke.edu/acad/intrel/bush/cheneymeetthepress.htm

Chesterman, Simon. (2004). *You, the People: The United Nations, Transitional Administration, and State-Building.* Oxford University Press: New York.

Chesterman, Simon. (2007) "Ownership in Theory and in Practice: Transfer of Authority in UN Statebuilding Operations." *Journal of Intervention and Statebuilding*, Vol. 1, No. 1, p. 3 — 26

Clark, Ian. (2007). *International Legitimacy and World Society.* Oxford: Oxford University Press.

Conference on Security and Cooperation in Europe (CSCE). (1990). *Charter of Paris for a New Europe, 21 November.* Paris.

Copeland, Dale. (2006). The constructivist challenge to structural realism. In: Guzzini, Stefano and Leander, Anna *Constructivism and International Politics.* New York: Routledge. pp. 1-20.

Cordesman, Anthony. (2010). "Past Failures and Future Transitions in Iraqi Reconstruction." Center for Strategic and International Studies, March 2nd.

(CPA) Coalition Provisional Authority. (2003). "Achieving the Vision to Restore Full Sovereignty to the Iraqi People – Strategic

Plan. Coalition Provisional Authority working Document, October 1st.

Crawford, Neta. (2006). How Previous Ideas Affect Later Ideas. In: Goodin, Robert and Tilly, Charles *The Oxford Handbook of Contextual Political Analysis*. New York: Oxford University Press. pp. 266-283.

Day, Graham and Freeman, Christopher. (2003). "Policekeeping is the Key: Rebuilding the International Security Architecture of Postwar Iraq." International *Affairs*, Vol. 79, No. 2, pp. 299-313.

Deflem, Mathieu and Sutohin, Suzanne. (2006). "Policing Post-War Iraq: Insurgency, Civilian Police, and the Reconstruction of Society." *Sociological Focus*, Vol. 39, No. 4, pp. 265-283.

Diamond, Larry. (2005). "Building Democracy After Conflict: Lessons from Iraq." *Journal of Democracy*, Vol. 16, No. 1, pp. 9-23.

DoA (Department of Army). (2006). Army Field Manual (FM) 3-24, *Counterinsurgency.* Available at: http://www.fas.org/irp/doddir/army/fm3-24fd.pdf

DoD (Department of Defence). (2002-2008). Office of the Joint Chief Staff, "Boots on Ground" data, multiple years.

Dobbins, James et al. (2005). *The UN's Role in Nation-Building: From the Congo to Iraq*. The Rand Corporation: Santa Monica.

Dodge, Toby. (2009). "Coming face to face with bloody reality: Liberal common sense and the ideological failure of the Bush doctrine in Iraq." *International Politics*, Vol. 46, pp. 253-275.

Dworkin, Gerald. (1971). "Paternalism" in Richard A. Wasserstrom (ed.) *Morality and the Law*. Belmont, CA: Wadsworth Publishing Company Inc.

Edelstain, Davis. (2004). "Occupational Hazards: Why Military Occupations Succeed or Fail." International Security, Vol. 29, No. 1, pp. 49-91.

Eikenberry, Karl. (2009). "Ambassador Eikenberry's Cables on U.S. Strategy in Afghanistan." The New York Times, November 9th. Available at http://documents.nytimes.com/eikenberry-s-memos-on-the-strategy-in-afghanistan#document/p1

Englebert, Pierre and Tull, Denis. (2008) 'Post Conflict Reconstruction in Africa: Flawed Ideas about Failed States.' *International Security*, Vol. 32, no. 4, p. 106-139.

Etzioni, Amitai. (2005). "Author's Response." *American Behavioural Scientist*, Vol. 48, No. 12, pp.1657-1665.

Etzioni, Amitai. (2009-10). "Bottom-up Nation Building." *Policy Review*, No. 158. Available at:
http://www.hoover.org/publications/policyreview/73084982.html

Fallows, James. (2004) "Blind into Baghdad." The Atlantic, January/February 2006. Available at:
http://www.theatlantic.com/magazine/archive/2004/01/blind-into-baghdad/2860/

Fearon, James and Laitin, David. (2004). "Neotrusteeship and the Problem of Weak States." *International Security*, Vol. 28, No. 4, pp. 5-43.

Feldman, Noah. (2004) *What We Owe Iraq*. Princeton: Princeton University Press.

Florini, Ann. (1996). "The Evolution of International Norms." *International Studies Quarterly*, Vol. 40, No. 3, pp. 363-389.

Flynn, Gregory and Farrell, Henry (1999). "Piecing Together the Democratic Peace: The CSCE, Norms, and the "Construction of Security in Post-Cold War Europe." *International Organization*, Vol. 53, No. 3, pp. 505-535.

Gilmore, Gerry. (2003). "Bulk of Iraq Reconstruction Monies 'Will Come from Iraqis,' Rumsfeld Says." American Forces Press Service, October 2nd. Available at: http://www.defense.gov/news/newsarticle.aspx?id=28388

Grindle, Merilee. (2002). "Good Enough Governance: Poverty Reduction and Reform in Developing Countries." Governance and Social Development Resource Centre. Available at: http://www.gsdrc.org/docs/open/HD32.pdf

Haddick, Robert. (2010). "This Week at War: Does the Pottery Barn Rule Still Apply?" Foreign Policy Magazine (Online), March 12th. Available at: http://www.foreignpolicy.com/articles/2010/03/12/this_week_at_ war_tear_down_the_wall

Halperin, M. H. (1993). 'Guaranteeing Democracy', *Foreign Policy*, No. 91, pp.105-122.

Hartmann, Michael. (2003). "International Judges and Prosecutors in Kosovo: A New Model for Post-Conflict Peacekeeping." United States Institute of Peace, Special Report 112, October 2003.

Hass, Richard. (2005). "The case for 'integration.'" CBS Money Watch, Fall 2005. Available at: http://findarticles.com/p/articles/mi_m2751/is_81/ai_n15753412/ Hehir, Aidan. (2009). The myth of the failed state and the war on terror. In: Chandler, David *Statebuilding and Intervention*. Cornwall: Routledge. pp. 72-98.

Hindess, B. (2002) "Neo-liberal citizenship." *Citizenship Studies*, Volume 6, Issue 2, pp. 127–143.

ICG (International Crisis Group). (2008). "Iraq After the Surge II: The Need for a New Political Strategy – Executive Summary and Recommendations." *Middle East Report*, No. 75, pp. i-36.

IISS (International Institute for Strategic Studies). (2005/2006). *The Military Balance*. London: Oxford University Press.

IISS (International Institute for Strategic Studies). (2007). *The Military Balance*. London: Oxford University Press.

IISS (International Institute for Strategic Studies). (2008). *The Military Balance*. London: Oxford University Press.

Iraqi Study Group. (2006). The United States Congressional Report, United States Institute of Peace.

Jenkins, Brian. (2009). "Afghanistan: A Marathon, Not a Prize Fight." RAND Corporation, December 1st. Available at: http://www.rand.org/commentary/2009/12/01/RAND.html

Jenkins, Darrell. (2007). "Phase Four: Applying History's Successful Nation Building Lessons in Iraq." USAWC Strategy Research Project, US Army War College.

Jones, Seth [et al]. (2005). *Establishing Law and Order After Conflict*. The RAND Corporation, Santa Monica.

Jones, Seth. (2010). "U.S. Strategy in Afghanistan." Before the Committee on Foreign Affairs, Subcommittee on Middle East and South Asia United States, House of Representatives, April 2nd. Available at:
http://www.rand.org/pubs/testimonies/2009/RAND_CT324.pdf

Katzenstein, P. (1996). *The Culture of National Security: Norms and Identities in World Politics*. New York: Columbia University Press.

Keane, Jack and Kagan, Frederick. (2006). "The Right Type of 'Surge.'" The Washington Post, December 27th. Available at: http://www.washingtonpost.com/wp-dyn/content/article/2006/12/26/AR2006122600773.html

Kerr, P.H. (1916). "Political Relations Between Advanced and Backward Peoples" in *An Introduction to the Study of International Relations*. London, Macmillan.

Kerton-Johnson, Nicholas. (2008) "Justifying the use of force in a post-9/11 world: striving for hierarchy in international society." *International Affairs*, Vol. 84, No. 5, pp.991-1007.

Koloski, Andrew and Kolasheski, John. (2009). "Thickening the Lines: Sons of Iraq, A Combat Multiplier." *Military Review*, January-February 2009, pp. 41-53.

Kratochwil, Friedrich. (2003). Constructing a new orthodoxy? Wendt's Social Theory of International Politics and the constructivist challenge. In: Guzzini, Stefano and Leander, Anna *Constructivism and International Politics*. New York: Routledge. pp. 21-47.

Krauthammer, Charles. (2004). "Democratic Realism." *The American Enterprise Institute Press*, Washington D.C.

Lauterpacht, Hersch. (1975). "International Law after the Second World War", in Elihu Lauterpacht (ed.), *International Law Being the Collected Papers of Hersch Lauterpacht (Vol. 2)*, Cambridge: Cambridge University Press, 1975, pp. 159-170.

Lansford, Tom. (2002). "Whither Lafayette? French Military Policy and the American Campaign in Afghanistan." *European Security*, vol. 11, no. 3, pp. 126-145.

Leverett, Flynt. (2007). "The Way Out: A roundtable discussion of our options for exiting Iraq." The American Prospect, July 10th. Available at:
http://www.prospect.org/cs/articles?article=the_way_out_of_iraq

Mann, James. (2004). *Rise of the Vulcans*. New York: Penguin Books.

Marx, Karl. (1853). *Karl Marx on Colonialism and Modernization* in Shlomo Avineri (ed.). Garden City, Anchor Books, 1969.

McMahon, Patrice. (2004/2005). "Rebuilding Bosnia: A Model to Emulate or to Avoid?" *Political Science Quarterly*, Vol. 119, No. 4, pp. 569-593.

Mertus, Julie. (2001). "Considering Elections in Kosovo: Lessons Learned from Bosnia." Carnegie Council, Carnegie Endowment for Peace, October 16th. Available at: http://www.cceia.org/resources/transcripts/194.html

Mill, John Stuart. (1859). *On Liberty* (Library of Liberal Arts Edition, 1956). New York: MacMillan.

Monten, Jonathan. (2005). "The Roots of the Bush Doctrine." *International Security*, Vol. 29, No. 4, pp. 112-156.

Morgenthau, Hans. (1945). "The Evil of Politics and the Ethics of Evil." Ethics, Volume 56, No. 1, p. 1-18.

Morgenthau, Hans. (1948). "The Twilight of International Morality." *Ethics*, Vol. 58, No. 2, pp. 79-99.

Narten, Jens. (2009). Dilemmas of promoting "local ownership": the case of postwar Kosovo. In: Paris, Roland and Sisk, Timothy *The Dilemmas of Statebuilding*. New York: Routledge. pp. 252-283.

Nkrumah, Kwame. (1962). *Towards Colonial Freedom: Africa and the Struggle Against World Imperialism*. London: Heinemann.

Norton-Taylor. "Afghanistan surge planned as shift to Kandahar proposed for UK soldiers." The Guardian, April 21st. Available at: http://www.guardian.co.uk/world/2010/apr/21/afghanistan-kandahar-soldiers-taliban

National Security Strategy of the United States of America (NSS). (2002). Office of the President of the United States of America.

Olesen, Thomas. (2005). "World Politics and Social Movements: The Janus Face of the Global Democratic Structure." *Global Society*, Vol. 19, No. 2

Oisin, Tansey. (2009). *Regime-Building: Democratization and International Administration.* New York: Oxford University Press.

Osterhammel, Jurgen (1995). *Colonialism: A Theoretical Overview*. 2nd ed. Princeton, NJ: Markus Weiner Publishers.

Owen, John. (2005). "Iraq and the Democratic Peace." *Foreign Affairs*, Vol. 84 Issue 6, pp. 122-127.

Paris, Roland. (2004). *At War's End: Building Peace after Civil Conflict*. Cambridge: Cambridge University Press.

Paris, Roland and Sisk, Timothy. (2009). Introduction: understanding the contradictions of postwar statebuilding. In: Prais, Roland and Sisk, Timothy *The Dilemmas of Statebuilding*. New York: Routledge. pp. 1-20.

Paul, Ron. (2007). Transcript: Republican Presidential Primary. University of New Hampshire, September 5th. Available at: http://www.foxnews.com/story/0,2933,295886,00.html

Payne, Rodger. (2007). "Neorealists as Critical Theorists: The Purpose of Foreign Policy Debate." *Perspectives on Politics*, Vol. 5, No. 3, pp.503-514.

Perito, Robert. (2006). "Policing Iraq: Protecting Iraqis from Criminal Violence." United States Institute of Peace. Available at: http://www.usip.org/resources/policing-iraq-protecting-iraqis-criminal-violence

Perriello, Tom. (2006). "Lessons from the Deployment of International Judges and Prosecutors in Kosovo." Prosecution Case Studies Series, the International Center for Transitional Justice.

Perry, William. (1991). "Desert Storm and Deterrence." *Foreign Affairs*, Vol. 70, Is. 4, pp. 66-82.

Pillai, Chad. (2009). "Tal Afar and Ar Ramadi: Grass Roots Reconstruction." *Military Review*, March-April 2009, pp. 33-39.

Press-Barnathan, Galia. (2004). "The War against Iraq and International Order: From Bull to Bush." *International Studies Review*, Vol. 6, No. 2, pp. 195-212.

Ragin, Charles. (2004). Turning the Tables: How Case-Oriented Research Challenges Variable-Oriented Research. In: Brady, Henry and Collier, David *Rethinking Social Inquiry*. New York, NY: Rowman & Littlefield Publishers, Inc.. pp. 123-138.

Rathmell, Andrew. (2005). "Planning post-conflict reconstruction in Iraq: what can we learn?" *International Affairs*, Vol. 81, No. 5, pp. 1013-1038.

Ricks, Thomas. (2006). *Fiasco*. London: Penguin Books.

Ricks, Thomas. (2010). "In Afghanistan, Petraeus will have difficulty replicating his Iraq success." The Washington Post, June 27th. Available at: http://www.washingtonpost.com/wp-dyn/content/article/2010/06/24/AR2010062402982.html

Robinson, Peter. (2009). "Resilient Force: Interview with Jack Keane." Hoover Digest, No. 3. Available at: http://www.hoover.org/publications/hoover-digest/article/5620

Rubin, Barnett. (2004). "(Re)Building Afghanistan: The Folly of Stateless Democracy." *Current History*, Vol. 103, Is. 672, pp. 165-170.

Rueschemeyer, Dietrich. (2006). Why and How Ideas Matter. In: Goodin, Robert and Tilly, Charles *The Oxford Handbook of Contextual Political Analysis*. New York: Oxford University Press. pp. 227-251.

Russett, Bruce. (1993). *Grasping the Democratic Peace.* Princeton: Princeton University Press.

Salhani, Claude. (2006) "Roundtable Forum: Iraq study Report – Responses to Iraq Study Report." International Affairs Forum, December 13th. Available at: http://www.ia-forum.org/Content/ForumContent.cfm?ForumTopicID=8

Sanger, David and Mazzetti, Mark. (2010). "New Estimate of Strength of Al Qaeda is Offered." The New York Times, June 30th. Available at: http://www.nytimes.com/2010/07/01/world/asia/01qaeda.html

Schmidt, Vivien. (2008). "Discursive Institutionalism: The Explanatory Power of Ideas and Discourse*." Annual Review of Political Science*, Vol. 11, pp. 303-326.

Simonsen, Sven Gunnar. (2006). "The Authoritarian Temptation in East Timor: Nationbuilding and the Need for Inclusive Governance." *Asian Survey*, Vol. 46, No. 4, pp. 575-596.

(SIGIR) Special Inspector General for Iraq Reconstruction. (2009). *Hard Lessons: The Iraq Reconstruction Experience.* US Independent Agencies and Commissions, the Office of the Special Inspector General for Iraq Reconstruction.

Starr, Fredrick. (2004). "U.S. Afghanistan Policy: It's Working." The Central Asia-Caucasus Institute, John Hopkins University.

Sumantra, Bose. (2002). *Bosnia after Dayton: Nationalist Partition and International Intervention.* London: Hurst and Co. Publishers.

Sweet, Lynn. (2006). "Iraq Study Group Report online. React from Durbin, Boehner, Pelosi, Reid, Schakowsky, Bayh, McCain, et al." Chicago Sun-Times, December 6th. Available at: http://blogs.suntimes.com/sweet/2006/12/iraq_study_group_repor t_online.html

Tripp, Charles (2007). *A History of Iraq*. 3rd ed. New York: Cambridge University Press.

United Nations Universal Declaration of Human Rights (UN UDHR). (1948). Available at: http://www.un.org/en/documents/udhr/index.shtml

United Nations Development Group (UNDG), World Bank and United Nations Development Programme. (2004). *Practical guide to multilateral needs assessments in post-conflict situations* (Washington DC: UN, Aug. 2004). Available at: http://www.unddr.org/tool_docs/PCNA.Tool_PostConflict_Needs_Assessment.pdf

United Nations. (1995). Supplement to an Agenda for Peace, Position Paper of the Secretary-General on the Occasion of the Fiftieth Anniversary of the United Nations, UN Doc A/50/60-S/1995/1. Accessed at: http://www.un.org/Docs/SG/agsupp.html

United Nations General Assembly. (1950). United Nations Department of Public Information. Available at: http://daccessddsny.un.org/doc/RESOLUTION/GEN/NR0/060/19/IMG/NR006019.pdf?OpenElement

(USIP) United States Institute of Peace. (2004). "Establishing the Rule of Law in Afghanistan." USIP Special Report No. 117, pp. 1-18.

Waltz, Kenneth. (1979). *Theory of International Politics*. New York: Addison-Wesley: McGraw-Hill.

Waltz, Kenneth. (1990). "Realist Thought and Neorealist Theory," *Journal of International Affairs*, Vol. 44, No 1, pp. 21-37.

Walzer, Michael. (1978). *Just and Unjust Wars*. London: Allen Lane.

Welch, Anthony. (2006). "Achieving Human Security after Intra-state Conflict: The Lessons of Kosovo." *Journal of Contemporary European Studies*, Vol. 14, No. 2, pp. 221-239.

Wendt, Alexander. (1992) "Anarchy is What States Make of It: The Social Construction of Power Politics." *International Organization*, Vol. 46, no. 2, pp. 391-425.

Wendt, Alexander. (1999). *Social Theory of International Politics*. New York: Cambridge University Press.

West, Bing. (2009). "Counterinsurgency Lessons from Iraq." *Military Review*, March-April 2009, pp. 2-12.

Westphal, David, and James Rosen. (2002). "Iraq swamps Democrats' major issues." *Sacramento Bee*, September 22. Available in NewsBank. Record Number SAC_0388937748.

Wheeler, Nicholas. (2000). *Saving Strangers: Humanitarian Intervention in International Society*. New York: Oxford University Press.

Wheeler, Nicholas. (2002). "Dying for 'Enduring Freedom': Accepting Responsibility for Civilian Casualties in the War against Terrorism." *International Relations*, Vol. 16, No. 2, pp. 205-225.

Wheeler, Nicholas and Dunne, Tim. (2001). "East Timor and the New Humanitarian Interventionism." *International affairs*, Vol. 77, No. 4, pp. 805-827.

Wilcke, Christoph. (2004). "Castles Built of Sand: US Governance and Exit Strategies in Iraq." *Middle East Report*, No. 232, pp. 4-13.

Wilson, Jeremy. (2006). "Law and Order in an Emerging Democracy: Lessons from the Reconstruction of Kosovo's Police and Justice Systems." *Annals of the American Academy of Political and Social Science*, Vol. 605, pp. 152-177.

Wight, Martin. (1991)."Western Values in International Relations." *In International Theory: The three Traditions* (edited by Gabriele Wight and Brian Porter). Leicester: Leicester University Press.

Woodward, Bob. (2008). *The War Within*. New York, Simon and Shuster.

Yousif, Bassam. (2006). "Coalition Economic Policies in Iraq: Motivations and Outcomes." *Third World Quarterly*, Vol. 27, No. 3, pp. 491-505.

About the Author

Ryan Sonneville has written about politics and war for the last decade. He completed his Masters of Science from the University of Edinburgh and his Masters in Education from the University of California, Davis.

He is a history teacher who lives in Sonoma County.